Ninja Foodi Digital Air Fry Oven Cookbook for Beginners

Delicious, Crispy & Easy-to-Prepare Digital Air Fry Oven Recipes for Fast & Healthy Meals

Jannah J. Kenzieman

Table of Contents

Introduction

The Ninja Foodi Digital Air Fryer Oven is one of the hottest kitchen gadgets available in the market. It is not just an electric oven. It is the combination of oven, air fryer, and toaster which makes Ninja Foodi is a multipurpose cooking appliance. It is loaded with 8 programmable functions like Air fry, Air Roast, Air Broil, Toast, keep warm, Dehydrate, Bake, and Bagel. Ninja is one of the strong competitors of instant pot for making advanced multipurpose cooking appliances. If you are a fried food lover, then Ninja foodi digital air fryer oven is one of the best choices for you. It makes your air fried food crispy and crunchy from the outside as well as juicy and tender from the inside. The device is an ideal choice for air fried dishes like French fries, chicken wings, onion rings, mozzarella sticks, and more.

The Ninja oven is one of the fast cooking appliances compare to another traditional oven. It cooks your food 60 % faster than others. In general, other oven takes 5 to 10 minutes to preheat the oven but Ninja oven takes only 60 seconds to preheat. The ninja oven is one of the power full oven runs on 1800 watt which makes daily cooking faster and easy. This hottest kitchen gadget makes your daily cooking easy. You can do almost all the cooking tasks using Ninja foodi oven.

The cookbook contains 100 different types of healthy and delicious recipes written from breakfast, main meal to deserts. All the recipes written in this cookbook are unique and choose from globally inspired dishes. The recipes are written in an easily understandable form and written with their preparation and cooking time. Every recipe written in this book ends with their actual nutritional value information. It helps to keep watch on daily calorie consumption. The cookbook also comes with 30 days meal plan which helps to change your eating habits towards healthy eating. There are lots of books available in the market on this topic thanks for choosing my book. I hope you love and enjoy the recipes written in this book.

Chapter 1: Ninja Foodi Digital Air Fryer Oven Basics

What is Ninja Foodi Digital Air Fryer Oven?

Ninja foodi digital air fryer is one of the advanced multipurpose all in one kitchen appliance. The main advantage of Ninja foodi digital air fryer oven is its different cooking functions. It is loaded with eight different functions like Air Fry, Air Roast, Air Broil, Keep Warm, Bake, Dehydrate, Toast and Bagel. You never need to buy separate cooking appliances for air frying, convection, and toasting purposes. It comes with a high-quality stainless-steel body and compact design with beautifully designed rounded corners. It saves your kitchen countertop space by just flip it up when the oven is not in use.

Ninja foodi oven comes with an extra-large capacity and capability to cook a large quantity of food into a single cooking cycle. It toasts 9 slices of bread, makes 13-inch pizza, and 6 chicken breasts at a time. The accessories like the air fryer basket, cooking rack, crumb tray, and non-stick sheet pan are dishwasher safe and you can easily remove it for the cleaning process. The crumb tray is set at the bottom inside position which protects the oven base from crumb, food dripping. The front flip lid and side-mounted control panel give an attractive look to your Ninja foodi oven. The control panel is simple to use and the functions given are simple to operate. The top rounded led display helps to show the information about cooking time followed by a cooking temperature. The rotating dial is bellowed the functions help to easily toggle between different cooking modes and also help to adjust the time and temperature settings.

Ninja Foodi allows you to enjoy your favorite fried food with very few fats and oil. It fries your French fries within a tablespoon of oil without compromising the taste and texture like deep-fried food. While comparing to a traditional oven your Ninja foodi air fryer oven cooks your food 60 % faster and it takes just 1 minute to preheat the oven. It automatically adjusts the convection fan speed while cooking your food and gives you even cooking results.

Control Panel Functions

Ninja foodi oven comes with an easily operate control panel system having display over rounded corners. The display helps to track the time and temperature settings, instead of the temperature display you will see the slice and darkness settings which are used while using bagel or toast mode settings.

Ninja foodi air fryer oven is loaded with various functions these function settings are as follows:

- Air Fry

Air fry is one of the healthiest cooking methods compare to deep frying. It fries your food using very little oil. A tablespoon of oil is enough to fry French fries, chicken wings, crispy beans, and more. It cooks your food faster and evenly by blowing hot air with the help of a convection fan rotating it at maximum speed. While using Air Fry functions setting you can set maximum period up to 1 hour and the temperature settings in between 250°F to 450°F.

- Air Roast

Ninja foodi allows you to use the air roast function with all kinds of sheet pan recipes. It not only roasts your favorite food but also makes it tender and gives a light brown texture over it. Using the air roast function, you can roast your favorite foods like veggies, steak, chicken, seafood, and more. While using Air Roast function settings you can set the maximum time up to 2 hours and the temperature settings in between 250°F to 450°F.

- Air Broil

Using Air Broil settings, you can broil or grill your chicken breast. It makes chicken breast juicy from the inside and given brown texture from the outside. While using these settings the maximum heat is produced from top heating elements and the convection fan runs at medium speed during the Air Broiling process. You can set a maximum period of up to 30 minutes and the temperature or darkness settings at high or low settings.

- Bake

Bake function allows you to bake your favorite cake, cookies, muffins, and more. During the baking process top and bottom heating elements produce even heat into the oven to get even baking results. While using the bake function you can set the maximum time up to 2 hours and the temperature settings in between 250°F to 450°F.

- Toast

While using toast settings the top and bottom heating elements produce even heat to toast your bread evenly from both sides. You can toast a maximum of 9 bread slice at once. During these settings, you never need to set time and temperature. These settings are automatically adjusted and depend on the number of bread slices and the darkness level of slices. You never need to flip the bread slices during the cooking cycle.

- Dehydrate

Using Dehydrate settings you can dehydrate your favorite food vegetable, meats, and fruit slices. Dehydrate is a long process in which food slices are dried due to dry heat. The Ninja Foodi Oven allows you to set the maximum time up to 12 hours and the ideal temperature settings are set in between 105°F to 195°F.

- Keep Warm

Using this function, you can maintain a certain temperature inside the oven to keep warm your food until you serve it. While using Keep Warm settings you can set the maximum time up to 2 hours.

- Bagel

While using these settings top and the lower heating elements produce dry heat to toast your bagel. Your Ninja foodi oven is capable to toast 6 bagel slices at a single cooking cycle. There is no need to set time and temperature settings. The machine will automatically adjust the time and temperature settings which depend on the number of slices place in the oven.

- Dialer

Ninja foodi oven is equipped with a multifunctional dial situated below the display functions. The dialer helps to easily navigate between the program list and also help to adjust the time and temperature settings as per recipe needs. You can use it to start and pause the oven. It is also used to set darkness levels and set the number of slices.

- LED Display

Ninja foodi air fryer oven comes with a round corner led display. It shows the time in hours and minutes and under the time it shows temperature in Fahrenheit. In front of time and temperature, the display shows preheat, slice, and dark level settings.

Benefits of Ninja Foodi Digital Air Fryer Oven

The Ninja foodi oven is one of the advanced cooking appliances that come with various benefits. All these benefits are given as follows:

1. Fast and Even Cooking

Compare to other traditional oven Ninja foodi digital air fryer oven cooks your food 60% faster. The best feature of the Ninja oven is it takes 60 seconds to preheat itself. Due to the larger size and fast cooking method, it cooks a family-size meal in less than 20 minutes. It is capable to cook large 13-inch pizza, 6 chicken breast, and 9 bread slices in a single cooking cycle respectively. While Air frying food the convection fan spins its maximum speed to blow hot air into the cooking area to give you faster and even cooking results.

2. Healthier cooking

Air frying function makes your daily cooking healthier. It consumes 75 to 85 % less fat and oils compare to the traditional deep-frying method. Air frying food is one of the healthiest choices for those who love fried food but worried about extra calorie intake.

3. Multipurpose Cooking Appliance

Ninja foodi oven is not just an oven it works as an air fryer, toaster, and more. It is loaded with various functions like Air Crisp, Air Roast, Air Broil, Dehydrate, Bake, Keep Warm, Bagel, and Toast. You never need to buy a separate appliance for different cooking tasks. The Ninja Foodi oven handles all these tasks by just touching the appropriate function button.

4. Easily Flip-up Store

Ninja foodi oven comes with a flip-up attachment which helps to store the oven backsplash position and save 50 % of your kitchen countertop space when the oven is not in use.

5. User-Friendly Operations

All the functions given over the control panel are easily understood and mention. You can easily use these functions with the help of a multipurpose dialer switch. The dialer allows you to navigate between these functions. It also uses to set desire time and temperature settings by just rotating the dial. When the oven is completely cool down then the display shows a FLIP message which indicates the oven is now ready to flip up.

6. Easy to clean

Ninja foodi oven assembles with easily removable accessories like an air fry basket, sheet pan, and crumb tray. You can remove all these accessories for cleaning. These accessories are dishwasher safe so you can place it into the dishwasher for cleaning. The back panel of the Ninja oven is easily removed so you can access the oven easily for a deep cleaning process.

Cleaning and Maintenance

The Ninja foodi digital air fryer oven is easy to clean you just need to follow the step by step instructions given below:

1. Before start, the cleaning process always makes sure the power cord is disconnecting from the main power switch. If the oven is hot, then allow it to cool down completely.
2. Remove all the accessories like air fry basket, sheet pan, and crumb tray from the main unit. Clean all the accessories with soapy water or you can clean it into the dishwasher. All the accessories that come with Ninja Foodi are dishwasher safe.

3. Then flip up the oven into its original storage position and press the push button to remove the back cover of the oven.
4. Now you can easily access the oven interior for cleaning. Take a soft cloth and clean the oven interior with the help of a damp cloth. Do not use harsh chemicals that may damage the oven interior. The main unit contains electric components so do not immerse it in water.
5. Make sure all the part is dry completely before assembling it into air fryer oven.
6. Place the back cover of the oven at its original position. Flip down the oven and place all the accessories in its original position. Flip the oven up position until next use.

Chapter 2: Breakfast

Healthy Tofu Egg Muffins

Preparation Time: 10 minutes
Cooking Time: 20 minutes
Serve: 12

Ingredients:

- 6 eggs
- ½ cup cheddar cheese, grated
- 6 oz smoked tofu, chopped
- 1 medium onion, chopped
- 1 leek, chopped
- ¼ tsp pepper
- ½ tsp salt

Directions:

1. Spray 12-cups muffin tray with cooking spray and set aside.
2. In a mixing bowl, whisk eggs with pepper and salt.
3. Add onion, leek, tofu, and cheese and stir well.
4. Pour egg mixture into the prepared muffin tray.
5. Select bake then set the temperature to 390 F and time to 20 minutes. Press start.
6. Once the oven is preheated then place muffin tray in the oven.
7. Serve and enjoy.

Nutritional Value (Amount per Serving):

- Calories 79
- Fat 4.6 g
- Carbohydrates 2.7 g
- Sugar 0.9 g
- Protein 7.2 g
- Cholesterol 87 mg

Baked Omelet

Preparation Time: 10 minutes

Cooking Time: 45 minutes

Serve: 4

Ingredients:

- 8 eggs
- 1 cup bell pepper, chopped
- ½ cup cheddar cheese, shredded
- ¾ cup ham, cooked & diced
- 1 cup milk
- ½ cup onion, chopped
- ½ tsp salt

Directions:

1. Spray baking pan with cooking spray and set aside.
2. In a bowl, whisk eggs with milk and salt.
3. Stir in bell pepper, onion, cheese, and ham.
4. Pour egg mixture into the prepared baking pan.
5. Select bake then set the temperature to 350 F and time to 45 minutes. Press start.
6. Once the oven is preheated then place baking pan in the oven.
7. Slice and serve.

Nutritional Value (Amount per Serving):

- Calories 270
- Fat 17 g
- Carbohydrates 8.4 g
- Sugar 5.6 g
- Protein 21.3 g
- Cholesterol 362 mg

French Toast Sticks

Preparation Time: 10 minutes
Cooking Time: 12 minutes
Serve: 6

Ingredients:

- 4 bread slices, cut each slice into 3 strips
- 1 tsp vanilla
- ¼ cup milk
- 1 tsp cinnamon
- 2 tbsp maple syrup
- 1 egg, lightly beaten
- 1 tbsp butter, melted

Directions:

1. In a bowl, whisk egg, vanilla, milk, cinnamon, butter, and maple syrup.
2. Spray air fryer basket with cooking spray and set aside.
3. Coat each bread piece with egg mixture and place in the air fryer basket.
4. Select air fry then set the temperature to 370 F and time to 12 minutes. Press start.
5. Once the oven is preheated the place air fryer basket into the top rails of the oven. After 8 minutes flip bread slices.
6. Serve and enjoy.

Nutritional Value (Amount per Serving):

- Calories 69
- Fat 3.1 g
- Carbohydrates 8.5 g
- Sugar 4.9 g
- Protein 1.8 g
- Cholesterol 33 mg

Bacon Egg Breakfast Casserole

Preparation Time: 10 minutes
Cooking Time: 45 minutes
Serve: 12

Ingredients:

- 12 eggs
- 1 cup cheddar cheese, shredded
- 4 oz cream cheese, cubed
- ½ lb bacon, cooked & crumbled
- 1 cup heavy cream
- ¼ tsp pepper
- ¼ tsp salt

Directions:

1. Spray casserole dish with cooking spray and set aside.
2. In a large bowl, whisk eggs with ½ cup cheddar cheese, heavy cream, pepper, and salt. Stir in cream cheese.
3. Pour egg mixture into the prepared casserole dish.
4. Select bake then set the temperature to 350 F and time to 35 minutes. Press start.
5. Once the oven is preheated then place casserole dish in the oven.
6. Sprinkle remaining cheese and bacon on top of casserole and bake for 10 minutes more.
7. Serve and enjoy.

Nutritional Value (Amount per Serving):

- Calories 271
- Fat 22.4 g
- Carbohydrates 1.3 g
- Sugar 0.4 g
- Protein 15.8 g
- Cholesterol 218 mg

Egg Sweet Potato Hash Muffins

Preparation Time: 10 minutes
Cooking Time: 20 minutes
Serve: 12

Ingredients:

- 12 eggs
- 1 small onion, diced
- 1 link chicken sausage, chopped
- ½ sweet potato, shredded
- 1 tsp everything bagel seasoning
- Pepper
- Salt

Directions:

1. Spray 12-cups muffin tray with cooking spray and set aside.
2. In a bowl, whisk eggs with pepper and salt.
3. Add onion, sausage, sweet potato, and bagel seasoning and stir well.
4. Pour egg mixture into the prepared muffin tray.
5. Select bake then set the temperature to 350 F and time to 20 minutes. Press start.
6. Once the oven is preheated then place muffin tray in the oven.
7. Serve and enjoy.

Nutritional Value (Amount per Serving):

- Calories 83
- Fat 5 g
- Carbohydrates 2.5 g
- Sugar 0.9 g
- Protein 7 g
- Cholesterol 170 mg

Soft & Fluffy Strawberry Donuts

Preparation Time: 10 minutes
Cooking Time: 17 minutes
Serve: 12

Ingredients:

- 2 eggs
- ½ cup strawberries, chopped
- 1 cup all-purpose flour
- ½ tsp vanilla
- 1 tsp baking powder
- ¾ cup sugar
- ½ cup buttermilk
- ¼ cup olive oil
- ½ tsp salt

Directions:

1. Spray donut pan with cooking spray and set aside.
2. In a bowl, whisk eggs, vanilla, baking powder, sugar, buttermilk, oil, and salt until well combined.
3. Add flour and stir until well combined.
4. Add strawberries and stir well.
5. Pour mixture into the prepared donut pan.
6. Select bake then set the temperature to 350 F and time to 17 minutes. Press start.
7. Once the oven is preheated then place donut pan in the oven.
8. Serve and enjoy.

Nutritional Value (Amount per Serving):

- Calories 138
- Fat 5.1 g
- Carbohydrates 21.7 g
- Sugar 13.4 g
- Protein 2.4 g
- Cholesterol 28 mg

Delicious Breakfast Potatoes

Preparation Time: 10 minutes
Cooking Time: 30 minutes
Serve: 6

Ingredients:

- 1 ½ lbs baby potatoes, quartered
- 1 tsp onion powder
- 2 tsp garlic powder
- 2 tbsp olive oil
- 1 green bell pepper, diced
- 1 red bell pepper, diced
- Pepper
- Salt

Directions:

1. Toss potatoes with olive oil in a mixing bowl.
2. Add remaining ingredients and toss well.
3. Transfer potato mixture to air fryer basket.
4. Select air fry then set the temperature to 400 F and time to 30 minutes. Press start.
5. Once the oven is preheated then place air fryer basket into the top rails of the oven. Stir potatoes 2-3 times.
6. Serve and enjoy.

Nutritional Value (Amount per Serving):

- Calories 122
- Fat 4.8 g
- Carbohydrates 17.8 g
- Sugar 2 g
- Protein 3.5 g
- Cholesterol 0 mg

Coconut Pineapple Oatmeal

Preparation Time: 10 minutes
Cooking Time: 35 minutes
Serve: 6

Ingredients:

- 2 eggs, lightly beaten
- 2 cups old fashioned oats
- ½ cup coconut flakes
- 1 cup pineapple, crushed
- ½ tsp vanilla
- 1/3 cup Greek yogurt
- 1/3 cup butter, melted
- ½ tsp baking powder
- 1/3 cup brown sugar
- ½ tsp salt

Directions:

1. Spray a baking dish with cooking spray and set aside.
2. In a mixing bowl, mix oats, baking powder, brown sugar, and salt.
3. In a separate bowl, whisk eggs with vanilla, milk, yogurt, butter.
4. Pour egg mixture into the oat mixture and mix until well combined.
5. Add coconut flakes and crushed pineapple and stir to combine.
6. Pour mixture into prepared baking dish.
7. Select bake then set the temperature to 350 F and time to 35 minutes. Press start.
8. Once the oven is preheated then place baking dish in the oven.
9. Serve and enjoy.

Nutritional Value (Amount per Serving):

- Calories 398
- Fat 17.6 g
- Carbohydrates 49.6 g
- Sugar 13.5 g
- Protein 9.8 g
- Cholesterol 83 mg

Banana Oatmeal Muffins

Preparation Time: 10 minutes
Cooking Time: 20 minutes
Serve: 12

Ingredients:

- 1 egg
- 1 tsp vanilla
- ¼ cup honey
- ¾ cup milk
- 1 cup banana, mashed
- ½ tsp cinnamon
- 1 tsp baking powder
- 2 ¼ cups old-fashioned oats
- ¼ tsp salt

Directions:

1. Spray 12-cups muffin tray with cooking spray and set aside.
2. In a mixing bowl, mix oats, cinnamon, baking powder, and salt and set aside.
3. In a separate bowl, whisk egg with vanilla, honey, milk, and mashed banana.
4. Add oat mixture into the egg mixture and mix until well combined.
5. Pour mixture into the prepared muffin tray.
6. Select bake then set the temperature to 350 F and time to 20 minutes. Press start.
7. Once the oven is preheated then place muffin tray in the oven.
8. Serve and enjoy.

Nutritional Value (Amount per Serving):

- Calories 103
- Fat 1.7 g
- Carbohydrates 19.9 g
- Sugar 8.2 g
- Protein 3.1 g
- Cholesterol 15 mg

Jalapeno Egg Muffins

Preparation Time: 10 minutes
Cooking Time: 15 minutes
Serve: 12

Ingredients:

- 10 eggs
- 1/3 cup bacon, cooked & chopped
- ½ cup cheddar cheese, shredded
- 1/3 cup cream cheese, softened
- 3 jalapeno peppers, chopped
- ½ tsp onion powder
- ½ tsp garlic powder
- Pepper
- Salt

Directions:

1. Spray 12-cups muffin tray with cooking spray and set aside.
2. In a bowl, whisk eggs with onion powder, garlic powder, pepper, and salt.
3. Add bacon, cheddar cheese, cream cheese, jalapeno peppers, and stir well.
4. Pour egg mixture into the prepared muffin tray.
5. Select bake then set the temperature to 400 F and time to 15 minutes. Press start.
6. Once the oven is preheated then place muffin tray in the oven.
7. Serve and enjoy.

Nutritional Value (Amount per Serving):

- Calories 96
- Fat 7.5 g
- Carbohydrates 1 g
- Sugar 0.5 g
- Protein 6.4 g
- Cholesterol 148 mg

Chapter 3: Poultry

Flavorful Chicken Wings

Preparation Time: 10 minutes
Cooking Time: 16 minutes
Serve: 6

Ingredients:

- 16 chicken wings, wash & pat dry
- 1 tbsp garlic salt
- ¾ cup brown sugar
- ½ tbsp pepper
- 2 tbsp garlic powder
- 1 tbsp chili powder
- 1 tbsp paprika
- ½ tbsp cayenne pepper
- 2 tbsp salt

Directions:

1. Spray air fryer basket with cooking spray.
2. In a small bowl, mix garlic salt, brown sugar, pepper, garlic powder, chili powder, paprika, cayenne, and salt.
3. Add chicken wings and spice mixture into the zip-lock bag, seal bag, and shake until chicken wings are well coated.
4. Arrange chicken wings to air fryer basket.
5. Select air fry then set the temperature to 400 F and time to 16 minutes. Press start.
6. Once the oven is preheated then place air fryer basket into the top rails of the oven. After 8 minutes flip chicken wings.
7. Serve and enjoy.

Nutritional Value (Amount per Serving):

- Calories 507
- Fat 29 g
- Carbohydrates 35 g

- Sugar 18.2 g
- Protein 26.7 g
- Cholesterol 103 mg

Nutritious Chicken & Veggies

Preparation Time: 10 minutes
Cooking Time: 15 minutes
Serve: 4

Ingredients:

- 1 lb chicken breasts, cut into bite-size pieces
- 1 tbsp Italian seasoning
- ½ tsp garlic powder
- ½ tsp chili powder
- 2 tbsp olive oil
- 2 garlic cloves, minced
- ½ onion, chopped
- 1 cup bell pepper, chopped
- 1 zucchini, chopped
- 1 cup broccoli florets
- Pepper
- Salt

Directions:

1. Add chicken, veggies, and remaining ingredients into the mixing bowl and toss well.
2. Spread chicken and vegetable mixture on a sheet pan.
3. Select air fry then set the temperature to 400 F and time to 15 minutes. Press start.
4. Once the oven is preheated then place sheet pan in the oven. Stir after 10 minutes.
5. Serve and enjoy.

Nutritional Value (Amount per Serving):

- Calories 321
- Fat 16.8 g
- Carbohydrates 8 g
- Sugar 3.8 g
- Protein 34.7 g
- Cholesterol 103 mg

Crispy & Juicy Chicken Drumsticks

Preparation Time: 10 minutes
Cooking Time: 25 minutes
Serve: 4

Ingredients:

- 4 chicken drumsticks
- 1 tsp chili powder
- 2 tsp smoked paprika
- 1 tbsp olive oil
- ½ tsp black pepper
- 1 tsp salt

Directions:

1. Coat chicken drumsticks with olive oil and rub with chili powder, paprika, pepper, and salt.
2. Arrange chicken drumsticks to air fryer basket.
3. Select air fry then set the temperature to 390 F and time to 25 minutes. Press start.
4. Once the oven is preheated then place air fryer basket into the top rails of the oven. Flip chicken drumsticks halfway through.
5. Serve and enjoy.

Nutritional Value (Amount per Serving):

- Calories 113
- Fat 6.4 g
- Carbohydrates 1.1 g
- Sugar 0.2 g
- Protein 12.9 g
- Cholesterol 40 mg

Crispy Chicken Thighs

Preparation Time: 10 minutes
Cooking Time: 22 minutes
Serve: 4

Ingredients:

- 4 chicken thighs
- ½ tsp onion powder
- ½ tsp oregano
- 1 tsp garlic powder
- 1 tsp paprika
- ½ tsp kosher salt

Directions:

1. Add chicken thighs and remaining ingredients into the zip-lock bag, seal bag and shake well.
2. Arrange chicken thighs onto the sheet pan.
3. Select air fry then set the temperature to 380 F and time to 22 minutes. Press start.
4. Once the oven is preheated then place sheet pan in the oven. Flip chicken thighs after 12 minutes.
5. Serve and enjoy.

Nutritional Value (Amount per Serving):

- Calories 398
- Fat 12.6 g
- Carbohydrates 10.4 g
- Sugar 1.1 g
- Protein 56.1 g
- Cholesterol 177 mg

Flavorful Chicken Fajitas

Preparation Time: 10 minutes
Cooking Time: 15 minutes
Serve: 8

Ingredients:

- 1 lb chicken breasts, boneless, skinless & cut into strips
- 1 tbsp olive oil
- 3 tbsp Fajita seasoning
- 1 onion, sliced
- 1 green bell pepper, cut into slices
- 1 yellow bell pepper, cut into slices
- 1 red bell pepper, cut into slices

Directions:

1. Add chicken and remaining ingredients into the mixing bowl and toss well.
2. Transfer chicken mixture to air fryer basket and spread well.
3. Select air fry then set the temperature to 390 F and time to 15 minutes. Press start.
4. Once the oven is preheated then place air fryer basket into the top rails of the oven. Stir halfway through.
5. Serve and enjoy.

Nutritional Value (Amount per Serving):

- Calories 154
- Fat 6.1 g
- Carbohydrates 7 g
- Sugar 2.8 g
- Protein 17 g
- Cholesterol 50 mg

Easy Buffalo Wings

Preparation Time: 10 minutes
Cooking Time: 25 minutes
Serve: 6

Ingredients:

- 1 lb chicken wings
- ¼ tsp paprika
- ¼ tsp garlic powder
- Pepper
- Salt
- For sauce:
- 1 cup buffalo sauce
- ¼ cup honey
- ¼ cup butter

Directions:

1. Toss chicken wings with paprika, garlic powder, pepper, and salt.
2. Arrange chicken wings to air fryer basket.
3. Select air fry then set the temperature to 350 F and time to 20 minutes. Press start.
4. Once the oven is preheated then place air fryer basket into the top rails of the oven. After 10 minutes flip chicken wings.
5. Meanwhile, melt butter in a pan over medium heat. Once butter is melted then add honey and stir until well combined.
6. Add buffalo sauce and stir well and cook over low heat for 5 minutes.
7. Transfer cooked chicken wings into the large bowl. Pour hot sauce over chicken wings and toss to coat.
8. Serve and enjoy.

Nutritional Value (Amount per Serving):

- Calories 268
- Fat 14.5 g
- Carbohydrates 12.5 g
- Sugar 11.8 g
- Protein 22 g
- Cholesterol 88 mg

Sesame Chicken

Preparation Time: 10 minutes
Cooking Time: 30 minutes
Serve: 2

Ingredients:

- 2 chicken breasts, boneless
- 1 tsp onion powder
- 1 tsp garlic powder
- ¼ tsp cayenne pepper
- 1 tbsp sweet paprika
- 2 tbsp sesame oil
- Pepper
- Salt

Directions:

1. In a small bowl, mix onion powder, garlic powder, cayenne pepper, paprika, pepper, and salt.
2. Brush chicken breasts with oil and rub with spice mixture.
3. Arrange chicken breasts onto the sheet pan.
4. Select air fry then set the temperature to 380 F and time to 30 minutes. Press start.
5. Once the oven is preheated then place sheet pan in the oven. Flip chicken after 20 minutes.
6. Serve and enjoy.

Nutritional Value (Amount per Serving):

- Calories 379
- Fat 12.6 g
- Carbohydrates 23.4 g
- Sugar 2.1 g
- Protein 42 g
- Cholesterol 147 mg

Tasty Chicken Nuggets

Preparation Time: 10 minutes
Cooking Time: 12 minutes
Serve: 4

Ingredients:

- 2 eggs, lightly beaten
- 1 lb chicken tenders, skinless & boneless
- 1 tsp herb & garlic seasoning
- 1 tbsp parmesan cheese, grated
- 2 oz breadcrumbs
- 2 oz potato chips, crushed
- Pepper
- Salt

Directions:

1. Spray air fryer basket with cooking spray and set aside.
2. Cut chicken into bite-size pieces.
3. In a bowl, mix breadcrumbs, crushed potato chips, cheese, herb & garlic seasoning, pepper, and salt.
4. In a separate bowl, add eggs and whisk well.
5. Dip chicken pieces into the egg then coat with breadcrumb mixture.
6. Arrange coated chicken pieces onto the air fryer basket.
7. Select air fry then set the temperature to 380 F and time to 12 minutes. Press start.
8. Once the oven is preheated then place air fryer basket into the top rails of the oven. After 6 minutes flip chicken nuggets.
9. Serve and enjoy.

Nutritional Value (Amount per Serving):

- Calories 380
- Fat 16.7 g
- Carbohydrates 17.4 g
- Sugar 1.1 g
- Protein 38.4 g
- Cholesterol 183 mg

Lemon Pepper Chicken Wings

Preparation Time: 10 minutes

Cooking Time: 16 minutes

Serve: 4

Ingredients:

- 1 lb chicken wings
- 1 tsp lemon pepper seasoning
- 2 tsp garlic salt
- 1 tbsp olive oil

Directions:

1. Toss chicken wings with oil, garlic salt, and lemon pepper seasoning.
2. Arrange chicken wings to air fryer basket.
3. Select air fry then set the temperature to 400 F and time to 16 minutes. Press start.
4. Once the oven is preheated then place air fryer basket into the top rails of the oven. After 8 minutes flip chicken wings.
5. Serve and enjoy.

Nutritional Value (Amount per Serving):

- Calories 345
- Fat 14.3 g
- Carbohydrates 9.6 g
- Sugar 8.8 g
- Protein 42.4 g
- Cholesterol 130 mg

Turkey Patties

Preparation Time: 10 minutes
Cooking Time: 30 minutes
Serve: 6

Ingredients:

- 1 lb ground turkey
- ¼ tsp cinnamon
- ½ tsp cayenne
- ½ tsp pepper
- 2 tsp fresh thyme
- 1 tbsp fresh sage
- 2 tbsp maple syrup
- Pepper
- Salt

Directions:

1. Line sheet pan with parchment paper and set aside.
2. Add all ingredients into the bowl and mix until well combined.
3. Make small patties from the mixture and place onto the prepared sheet pan.
4. Select bake then set the temperature to 350 F and time to 30 minutes. Press start.
5. Once the oven is preheated then place sheet pan in the oven.
6. Serve and enjoy.

Nutritional Value (Amount per Serving):

- Calories 168
- Fat 8.4 g
- Carbohydrates 5.2 g
- Sugar 4 g
- Protein 20.8 g
- Cholesterol 77 mg

Healthy Meatballs

Preparation Time: 10 minutes
Cooking Time: 25 minutes
Serve: 6

Ingredients:

- 1 egg, lightly beaten
- 1 lb ground turkey
- ¼ tsp pepper
- ½ tsp onion powder
- ½ tsp garlic powder
- ½ tsp dried oregano
- ½ tsp dried basil
- 1 tbsp parsley, minced
- 2 tbsp milk
- ½ cup parmesan cheese, grated
- ½ cup breadcrumbs
- ½ tsp salt

Directions:

1. Line sheet pan with parchment paper and set aside.
2. Add all ingredients into the mixing bowl and mix until well combined.
3. Make balls from meat mixture and place onto the prepared sheet pan.
4. Select bake then set the temperature to 400 F and time to 25 minutes. Press start.
5. Once the oven is preheated then place sheet pan in the oven.
6. Serve and enjoy.

Nutritional Value (Amount per Serving):

- Calories 248
- Fat 12.6 g
- Carbohydrates 7.3 g
- Sugar 1 g
- Protein 27.1 g
- Cholesterol 115 mg

Healthy Chicken Patties

Preparation Time: 10 minutes
Cooking Time: 25 minutes
Serve: 5

Ingredients:

- 1 egg, lightly beaten
- 1 lb ground chicken
- 1 tsp garlic, minced
- ½ cup onion, minced
- ¾ cup breadcrumbs
- ½ cup cheddar cheese, grated
- 1 cup carrot, grated
- 1 cup cauliflower, grated
- Pepper
- Salt

Directions:

1. Line sheet pan with parchment paper and set aside.
2. Add all ingredients into the bowl and mix until well combined.
3. Make small patties from the mixture and place onto the prepared sheet pan.
4. Select bake then set the temperature to 400 F and time to 25 minutes. Press start.
5. Once the oven is preheated then place sheet pan in the oven.
6. Serve and enjoy.

Nutritional Value (Amount per Serving):

- Calories 314
- Fat 12.2 g
- Carbohydrates 16.4 g
- Sugar 3.2 g
- Protein 33.1 g
- Cholesterol 125 mg

Ranch Chicken Wings

Preparation Time: 10 minutes
Cooking Time: 50 minutes
Serve: 4

Ingredients:

- 2 lbs chicken wings
- 2 tsp dried dill spice
- 1 tbsp chipotle spice
- 2 tbsp onion powder
- 2 tbsp garlic powder
- 1 tsp pepper
- ½ tbsp kosher salt

Directions:

1. Toss chicken wings and remaining ingredients into the mixing bowl and toss well.
2. Arrange chicken wings to air fryer basket.
3. Select bake then set the temperature to 400 F and time to 50 minutes. Press start.
4. Once the oven is preheated then place air fryer basket into the top rails of the oven. After 30 minutes flip chicken wings.
5. Serve and enjoy.

Nutritional Value (Amount per Serving):

- Calories 458
- Fat 16.9 g
- Carbohydrates 6.2 g
- Sugar 2.2 g
- Protein 66.7 g
- Cholesterol 202 mg

Simple Turkey Meatballs

Preparation Time: 10 minutes
Cooking Time: 20 minutes
Serve: 6

Ingredients:

- 1 egg
- 1 ½ lbs ground turkey
- 2 tbsp Italian seasoning
- 1 cup fresh parsley, chopped
- 1/3 cup almond flour
- Pepper
- Salt

Directions:

1. Line sheet pan with parchment paper and set aside.
2. Add all ingredients into the mixing bowl and mix until well combined.
3. Make balls from meat mixture and place onto the prepared sheet pan.
4. Select bake then set the temperature to 400 F and time to 20 minutes. Press start.
5. Once the oven is preheated then place sheet pan in the oven.
6. Serve and enjoy.

Nutritional Value (Amount per Serving):

- Calories 285
- Fat 17.8 g
- Carbohydrates 2.5 g
- Sugar 0.8 g
- Protein 33.6 g
- Cholesterol 146 mg

Juicy & Tasty Chicken Breasts

Preparation Time: 10 minutes

Cooking Time: 10 minutes

Serve: 2

Ingredients:

- 2 chicken breasts, skinless & boneless
- 1 tbsp olive oil
- ¼ tsp garlic powder
- ¼ tsp onion powder
- ¼ tsp paprika
- Pepper
- Salt

Directions:

1. In a small bowl, mix garlic powder, onion powder, paprika, pepper, and salt.
2. Brush chicken breasts with oil and rub with spice mixture.
3. Arrange chicken breasts onto the sheet pan.
4. Select bake then set the temperature to 400 F and time to 10 minutes. Press start.
5. Once the oven is preheated then place sheet pan in the oven.
6. Serve and enjoy.

Nutritional Value (Amount per Serving):

- Calories 340
- Fat 17.9 g
- Carbohydrates 0.7 g
- Sugar 0.2 g
- Protein 42.4 g
- Cholesterol 130 mg

Chapter 4: Beef, Pork & Lamb

Tasty Steak Bites

Preparation Time: 10 minutes
Cooking Time: 15 minutes
Serve: 6

Ingredients:

- 2 lbs beef, cut into bite-size pieces
- 2 tbsp Worcestershire sauce
- 2 lbs mushrooms, sliced
- Pepper
- Salt

Directions:

1. Toss beef pieces with Worcestershire sauce, mushrooms, pepper, and salt and spread onto the sheet pan.
2. Select air fry then set the temperature to 400 F and time to 15 minutes. Press start.
3. Once the oven is preheated then place sheet pan in the oven. Stir halfway through.
4. Serve and enjoy.

Nutritional Value (Amount per Serving):

- Calories 318
- Fat 9.9 g
- Carbohydrates 6 g
- Sugar 3.6 g
- Protein 50.6 g
- Cholesterol 135 mg

Beef & Broccoli

Preparation Time: 10 minutes
Cooking Time: 15 minutes
Serve: 2

Ingredients:

- 1 lb broccoli florets
- ½ lb steak, cut into strips
- 1 tsp ginger garlic paste
- 2 tbsp sesame oil
- 2 tbsp soy sauce
- 1/3 cup oyster sauce

Directions:

1. Add meat pieces and remaining ingredients into the mixing bowl and let marinate for 1 hour.
2. Add marinated meat pieces and broccoli florets into the air fryer basket.
3. Select air fry then set the temperature to 350 F and time to 15 minutes. Press start.
4. Once the oven is preheated then place air fryer basket into the top rails of the oven. Stir halfway through.
5. Serve and enjoy.

Nutritional Value (Amount per Serving):

- Calories 437
- Fat 20.1 g
- Carbohydrates 17.5 g
- Sugar 4.1 g
- Protein 48.5 g
- Cholesterol 102 mg

Parmesan Beef Meatballs

Preparation Time: 10 minutes
Cooking Time: 20 minutes
Serve: 6

Ingredients:

- 1 egg, lightly beaten
- 2 tbsp garlic, minced
- 3 tbsp breadcrumbs
- 1 tsp dried parsley
- ½ cup parmesan cheese, grated
- 1 lb ground beef
- Pepper
- Salt

Directions:

1. Line sheet pan with parchment paper and set aside.
2. Add all ingredients into the mixing bowl and mix until well combined.
3. Make balls from meat mixture and place onto the prepared sheet pan.
4. Select bake then set the temperature to 375 F and time to 20 minutes. Press start.
5. Once the oven is preheated then place sheet pan in the oven.
6. Serve and enjoy.

Nutritional Value (Amount per Serving):

- Calories 269
- Fat 11.6 g
- Carbohydrates 3.4 g
- Sugar 0.3 g
- Protein 32.5 g
- Cholesterol 115 mg

Juicy Baked Burger Patties

Preparation Time: 10 minutes
Cooking Time: 15 minutes
Serve: 12

Ingredients:

- 3 lbs ground beef
- 1 tsp Tabasco
- 1 tbsp yellow mustard
- 2 tsp Worcestershire sauce
- ½ tsp granulated garlic
- Pepper
- Salt

Directions:

1. Line sheet pan with parchment paper and set aside.
2. Add all ingredients into the bowl and mix until well combined.
3. Make small patties from the mixture and place onto the prepared sheet pan.
4. Select bake then set the temperature to 425 F and time to 15 minutes. Press start.
5. Once the oven is preheated then place sheet pan in the oven.
6. Serve and enjoy.

Nutritional Value (Amount per Serving):

- Calories 370
- Fat 9.8 g
- Carbohydrates 0.4 g
- Sugar 0.1 g
- Protein 65.4 g
- Cholesterol 197 mg

Ranch Pork Chops

Preparation Time: 10 minutes
Cooking Time: 30 minutes
Serve: 6

Ingredients:

- 6 pork chops, boneless
- 1 tsp dried parsley
- 1 oz dry ranch seasoning
- ¼ cup olive oil

Directions:

1. Place pork chops into the baking pan.
2. Mix parsley, ranch seasoning, and oil and pour over pork chops.
3. Select bake then set the temperature to 425 F and time to 30 minutes. Press start.
4. Once the oven is preheated then place baking pan in the oven.
5. Serve and enjoy.

Nutritional Value (Amount per Serving):

- Calories 328
- Fat 28.3 g
- Carbohydrates 0 g
- Sugar 0 g
- Protein 18 g
- Cholesterol 69 mg

Easy Pork Ribs

Preparation Time: 10 minutes
Cooking Time: 30 minutes
Serve: 8

Ingredients:

- 2 lbs pork ribs, boneless
- 1 tbsp onion powder
- 1 ½ tbsp garlic powder
- Pepper
- Salt

Directions:

1. Rub pork ribs with onion powder, garlic powder, pepper, and salt and place into the sheet pan.
2. Select bake then set the temperature to 350 F and time to 30 minutes. Press start.
3. Once the oven is preheated then place sheet pan in the oven.
4. Serve and enjoy.

Nutritional Value (Amount per Serving):

- Calories 318
- Fat 20.1 g
- Carbohydrates 1.9 g
- Sugar 0.7 g
- Protein 30.4 g
- Cholesterol 117 mg

Lamb Meatballs

Preparation Time: 10 minutes
Cooking Time: 20 minutes
Serve: 4

Ingredients:

- 1 egg, lightly beaten
- 1 lb ground lamb
- 3 tbsp olive oil
- ¼ tsp red pepper flakes, crushed
- ½ tsp pepper
- 1 tsp ground cumin
- 2 tsp oregano, chopped
- 2 tbsp parsley, chopped
- 1 tbsp garlic, minced
- 1 tsp kosher salt

Directions:

1. Line sheet pan with parchment paper and set aside.
2. Add all ingredients into the mixing bowl and mix until well combined.
3. Make balls from meat mixture and place onto the prepared sheet pan.
4. Select bake then set the temperature to 425 F and time to 20 minutes. Press start.
5. Once the oven is preheated then place sheet pan in the oven.
6. Serve and enjoy.

Nutritional Value (Amount per Serving):

- Calories 326
- Fat 20.2 g
- Carbohydrates 1.8 g
- Sugar 0.2 g
- Protein 33.6 g
- Cholesterol 143 mg

Greek Lamb Chops

Preparation Time: 10 minutes
Cooking Time: 15 minutes
Serve: 4

Ingredients:

- 8 lamb loin chops
- 2 tsp dried herb de Provence
- 1 tsp garlic, minced
- 2 tbsp olive oil
- 2 tbsp Dijon mustard
- Pepper
- Salt

Directions:

1. In a small bowl, mix herb de Provence, garlic, oil, Dijon mustard, pepper, and salt.
2. Brush lamb chops with herb de Provence mixture and place onto the sheet pan.
3. Select bake then set the temperature to 425 F and time to 15 minutes. Press start.
4. Once the oven is preheated then place sheet pan in the oven.
5. Serve and enjoy.

Nutritional Value (Amount per Serving):

- Calories 66
- Fat 7.3 g
- Carbohydrates 0.7 g
- Sugar 0.1 g
- Protein 0.4 g
- Cholesterol 0 mg

Parmesan Pork Chops

Preparation Time: 10 minutes
Cooking Time: 20 minutes
Serve: 4

Ingredients:

- 2 eggs, lightly beaten
- 4 pork chops, boneless
- 1/4 cup parmesan cheese, grated
- 1 cup almond flour
- 1 tbsp garlic powder
- 1/2 tbsp black pepper
- 1 tbsp onion powder
- 1/2 tsp sea salt

Directions:

1. In a bowl, mix almond flour, cheese, onion powder, garlic powder, pepper, and salt.
2. Whisk eggs in a shallow dish.
3. Dip pork chops into the egg then coat with almond flour mixture.
4. Place coated pork chops to air fryer basket.
5. Select air fry then set the temperature to 350 F and time to 20 minutes. Press start.
6. Once the oven is preheated then place air fryer basket into the top rails of the oven.
7. Serve and enjoy.

Nutritional Value (Amount per Serving):

- Calories 485
- Fat 37 g
- Carbohydrates 9.1 g
- Sugar 2.5 g
- Protein 30.1 g
- Cholesterol 160 mg

Beef Burger Patties

Preparation Time: 10 minutes
Cooking Time: 45 minutes
Serve: 4

Ingredients:

- 10 oz ground beef
- 1 tsp garlic puree
- 1 oz cheddar cheese
- 1 tsp mixed herbs
- 1 tsp mustard
- 1 tsp tomato puree
- 1 tsp basil
- Pepper
- Salt

Directions:

1. Line sheet pan with parchment paper and set aside.
2. Add all ingredients into the bowl and mix until well combined.
3. Make small patties from the mixture and place onto the prepared sheet pan.
4. Select air fry then set the temperature to 390 F and time to 45 minutes. Press start.
5. Once the oven is preheated then place sheet pan in the oven. Flip patties after 25 minutes.
6. Serve and enjoy.

Nutritional Value (Amount per Serving):

- Calories 174
- Fat 7.1 g
- Carbohydrates 0.8 g
- Sugar 0.2 g
- Protein 24.5 g
- Cholesterol 75 mg

Flavorful Beef Fajitas

Preparation Time: 10 minutes
Cooking Time: 8 minutes
Serve: 4

Ingredients:

- 1 lb steak, sliced
- 1 green bell peppers, sliced
- 1 tsp garlic powder
- 1 tsp smoked paprika
- 1 tsp cumin
- 1 yellow bell peppers, sliced
- 1/2 tbsp chili powder
- 3 tbsp olive oil
- Pepper
- Salt

Directions:

1. In a large bowl, toss sliced steak with remaining ingredients and spread onto a sheet pan.
2. Select air fry then set the temperature to 390 F and time to 8 minutes. Press start.
3. Once the oven is preheated then place sheet pan in the oven.
4. Serve and enjoy.

Nutritional Value (Amount per Serving):

- Calories 345
- Fat 16.7 g
- Carbohydrates 6.1 g
- Sugar 3 g
- Protein 42 g
- Cholesterol 102 mg

Herb Lamb Chops

Preparation Time: 10 minutes
Cooking Time: 8 minutes
Serve: 4

Ingredients:

- 1 lb lamb chops
- 2 tbsp fresh lemon juice
- 2 tbsp olive oil
- 1 tsp coriander
- 1 tsp oregano
- 1 tsp thyme
- 1 tsp rosemary
- 1 tsp salt

Directions:

1. Add lamb chops and remaining ingredients into the zip-lock bag, seal bag and shake well and place in the refrigerator for overnight.
2. Place marinated lamb chops in the air fryer basket.
3. Select air fry then set the temperature to 390 F and time to 8 minutes. Press start.
4. Once the oven is preheated then place air fryer basket into the top rails of the oven.
5. Serve and enjoy.

Nutritional Value (Amount per Serving):

- Calories 275
- Fat 15 g
- Carbohydrates 0.9 g
- Sugar 0.2 g
- Protein 32 g
- Cholesterol 101 mg

Easy Mustard Lamb Chops

Preparation Time: 10 minutes
Cooking Time: 15 minutes
Serve: 4

Ingredients:

- 8 lamb chops
- 1 1/2 tbsp Dijon mustard
- 1 1/2 tbsp lemon juice
- 1/2 tsp olive oil
- Pepper
- Salt

Directions:

1. In a small bowl, mix mustard, lemon juice, and olive oil.
2. Brush lamb chops with mustard mixture and place into the air fryer basket.
3. Select air fry then set the temperature to 390 F and time to 15 minutes. Press start.
4. Once the oven is preheated then place air fryer basket into the top rails of the oven. Flip lamb chops halfway through.
5. Serve and enjoy.

Nutritional Value (Amount per Serving):

- Calories 325
- Fat 13.5 g
- Carbohydrates 0.5 g
- Sugar 0.2 g
- Protein 49.1 g
- Cholesterol 153 mg

Tasty Beef Tips

Preparation Time: 10 minutes
Cooking Time: 12 minutes
Serve: 4

Ingredients:

- 1 lb steak, cut into 1-inch cubes
- 1 tsp garlic powder
- 2 tbsp coconut aminos
- 2 tsp rosemary, crushed
- 1 tsp smoked paprika
- 2 tsp onion powder
- Pepper
- Salt

Directions:

1. Add meat and remaining ingredients into the bowl and mix well and let it sit for 10 minutes.
2. Transfer steak cubes to air fryer basket.
3. Select air fry then set the temperature to 380 F and time to 12 minutes. Press start.
4. Once the oven is preheated then place air fryer basket into the top rails of the oven. Stir halfway through.
5. Serve and enjoy.

Nutritional Value (Amount per Serving):

- Calories 245
- Fat 6 g
- Carbohydrates 3.7 g
- Sugar 0.7 g
- Protein 41.3 g
- Cholesterol 102 mg

Herb Lamb Cutlets

Preparation Time: 10 minutes
Cooking Time: 30 minutes
Serve: 4

Ingredients:

- 4 lamb cutlets
- 2 garlic cloves, minced
- 1/2 tbsp oregano, chopped
- 1/2 tbsp basil, chopped
- 1 tsp olive oil
- 1/2 tbsp chives, chopped
- 2 tbsp mustard
- Pepper
- Salt

Directions:

1. Add lamb cutlets and remaining ingredients to the mixing bowl and coat well.
2. Place lamb cutlets into to air fryer basket.
3. Select air fry then set the temperature to 380 F and time to 30 minutes. Press start.
4. Once the oven is preheated then place air fryer basket into the top rails of the oven. Flip lamb cutlets halfway through.
5. Serve and enjoy.

Nutritional Value (Amount per Serving):

- Calories 200
- Fat 9.1 g
- Carbohydrates 3 g
- Sugar 0.4 g
- Protein 25.5 g
- Cholesterol 77 mg

Chapter 5: Fish & Seafood

Parmesan Shrimp

Preparation Time: 10 minutes
Cooking Time: 12 minutes
Serve: 4

Ingredients:

- 1 lb shrimp, peeled & deveined
- 2 tbsp fresh parsley, minced
- 2 tbsp parmesan cheese, grated
- 1/8 tsp garlic powder
- 2 tbsp olive oil
- ¼ tsp pepper
- ½ tsp salt

Directions:

1. In a mixing bowl, toss shrimp with remaining ingredients and transfer to the air fryer basket.
2. Select air fry then set the temperature to 400 F and time to 12 minutes. Press start.
3. Once the oven is preheated then place air fryer basket into the top rails of the oven. Stir shrimp halfway through.
4. Serve and enjoy.

Nutritional Value (Amount per Serving):

- Calories 206
- Fat 9 g
- Carbohydrates 2 g
- Sugar 0 g
- Protein 27 g
- Cholesterol 240 mg

Easy Tuna Cakes

Preparation Time: 10 minutes
Cooking Time: 12 minutes
Serve: 12

Ingredients:

- 2 eggs, lightly beaten
- 2 cans of tuna, drained
- ½ tsp black pepper
- ½ onion, diced
- 2 tbsp fresh lemon juice
- ¼ cup mayonnaise
- ½ cup breadcrumbs
- ½ tsp pepper
- ½ tsp salt

Directions:

1. Line sheet pan with parchment paper and set aside.
2. Add all ingredients into the bowl and mix until well combined.
3. Make small patties from the mixture and place onto the prepared sheet pan.
4. Select air fry then set the temperature to 375 F and time to 12 minutes. Press start.
5. Once the oven is preheated then place sheet pan in the oven. Flip patties halfway through.
6. Serve and enjoy.

Nutritional Value (Amount per Serving):

- Calories 84
- Fat 5 g
- Carbohydrates 4 g
- Sugar 1 g
- Protein 5 g
- Cholesterol 39 mg

Quick & Easy Shrimp Boil

Preparation Time: 10 minutes
Cooking Time: 8 minutes
Serve: 6

Ingredients:

- 1 lb shrimp, peeled & deveined
- 2 tbsp fresh parsley, chopped
- 12 oz smoked sausage, sliced
- 2 tbsp old bay seasoning
- 1 tbsp garlic, minced
- ½ cup butter, melted
- 3 ears corn, cut into 3-4 pieces & boiled
- 1 lb baby potatoes, boiled & sliced

Directions:

1. Add shrimp and remaining ingredients into the large bowl and toss well.
2. Transfer shrimp mixture to air fryer basket.
3. Select air fry then set the temperature to 400 F and time to 8 minutes. Press start.
4. Once the oven is preheated then place air fryer basket into the top rails of the oven. Stir shrimp halfway through.
5. Serve and enjoy.

Nutritional Value (Amount per Serving):

- Calories 392
- Fat 21 g
- Carbohydrates 31 g
- Sugar 4 g
- Protein 23 g
- Cholesterol 207 mg

Shrimp with Veggies

Preparation Time: 10 minutes
Cooking Time: 15 minutes
Serve: 4

Ingredients:

- 1 lb shrimp, peeled & deveined
- ¼ cup parmesan cheese, grated
- 1 tbsp Italian seasoning
- 1 tbsp garlic, minced
- 1 tbsp olive oil
- 1 bell pepper, sliced
- 1 zucchini, sliced
- Pepper
- Salt

Directions:

1. Add shrimp and remaining ingredients into the mixing bowl and toss well.
2. Transfer shrimp mixture to air fryer basket.
3. Select air fry then set the temperature to 350 F and time to 15 minutes. Press start.
4. Once the oven is preheated then place air fryer basket into the top rails of the oven. Stir halfway through.
5. Serve and enjoy.

Nutritional Value (Amount per Serving):

- Calories 346
- Fat 15.6 g
- Carbohydrates 6.7 g
- Sugar 2.7 g
- Protein 38.9 g
- Cholesterol 271 mg

Shrimp Fajitas

Preparation Time: 10 minutes
Cooking Time: 22 minutes
Serve: 12

Ingredients:

- 1 lb shrimp
- 2 tbsp fajita seasoning
- ½ cup onion, sliced
- 1 green bell pepper, sliced
- 1 red bell pepper, sliced
- 1 tbsp olive oil

Directions:

1. Toss shrimp with remaining ingredients into the large bowl and transfer to the air fryer basket.
2. Select air fry then set the temperature to 390 F and time to 22 minutes. Press start.
3. Once the oven is preheated then place air fryer basket into the top rails of the oven. Stir after 12 minutes.
4. Serve and enjoy.

Nutritional Value (Amount per Serving):

- Calories 68
- Fat 1.9 g
- Carbohydrates 3.6 g
- Sugar 1.2 g
- Protein 8.9 g
- Cholesterol 80 mg

Delicious Crab Cakes

Preparation Time: 10 minutes
Cooking Time: 10 minutes
Serve: 4

Ingredients:

- 8 oz crab meat
- 1 tsp old bay seasoning
- 1 tbsp Dijon mustard
- 2 tbsp breadcrumbs
- 2 tbsp mayonnaise
- 2 green onion, chopped
- ¼ cup bell pepper, chopped

Directions:

1. Line sheet pan with parchment paper and set aside.
2. Add all ingredients into the bowl and mix until well combined.
3. Make four patties from the mixture and place onto the prepared sheet pan.
4. Select air fry then set the temperature to 370 F and time to 10 minutes. Press start.
5. Once the oven is preheated then place sheet pan in the oven.
6. Serve and enjoy.

Nutritional Value (Amount per Serving):

- Calories 124
- Fat 6 g
- Carbohydrates 5 g
- Sugar 1 g
- Protein 12 g
- Cholesterol 27 mg

Easy Cajun Shrimp with Veggies

Preparation Time: 10 minutes
Cooking Time: 20 minutes
Serve: 4

Ingredients:

- 1 lb shrimp, peeled
- 2 tbsp olive oil
- 1 bell pepper, cut into 1-inch pieces
- 1 yellow squash, sliced into ¼-inch thick
- 1 zucchini, sliced
- 6 oz turkey sausage, cooked & sliced
- 1 tbsp Cajun seasoning
- ¼ tsp kosher salt

Directions:

1. Toss shrimp with remaining ingredients into the large bowl and transfer to the air fryer basket.
2. Select air fry then set the temperature to 400 F and time to 8 minutes. Press start.
3. Once the oven is preheated then place air fryer basket into the top rails of the oven. Stir 2 times.
4. Serve and enjoy

Nutritional Value (Amount per Serving):

- Calories 285
- Fat 14 g
- Carbohydrates 8 g
- Sugar 3 g
- Protein 31 g
- Cholesterol 205 mg

Rosemary Garlic Shrimp

Preparation Time: 10 minutes

Cooking Time: 10 minutes

Serve: 4

Ingredients:

- 1 lb shrimp, peeled and deveined
- 1/2 tbsp fresh rosemary, chopped
- 2 garlic cloves, minced
- 1 tbsp olive oil
- Pepper
- Salt

Directions:

1. Add shrimp and remaining ingredients in a large bowl and toss well.
2. Transfer shrimp mixture to a sheet pan.
3. Select bake then set the temperature to 400 F and time to 10 minutes. Press start.
4. Once the oven is preheated then place sheet pan in the oven.
5. Serve and enjoy.

Nutritional Value (Amount per Serving):

- Calories 168
- Fat 5.5 g
- Carbohydrates 2.5 g
- Sugar 0 g
- Protein 26 g
- Cholesterol 239 mg

Easy Shrimp Casserole

Preparation Time: 10 minutes

Cooking Time: 8 minutes

Serve: 4

Ingredients:

- 1 lb shrimp, peeled and deveined
- 1/2 cup breadcrumbs
- 1/4 cup butter, melted
- 2 tbsp white wine
- 1 tbsp garlic, minced
- 2 tbsp fresh parsley, chopped
- Pepper
- Salt

Directions:

1. Spray a baking dish with cooking spray and set aside.
2. Add shrimp into the large bowl.
3. Pour remaining ingredients over shrimp and toss well.
4. Pour shrimp mixture into the baking dish.
5. Select bake then set the temperature to 350 F and time to 8 minutes. Press start.
6. Once the oven is preheated then place baking dish in the oven.
7. Serve and enjoy.

Nutritional Value (Amount per Serving):

- Calories 300
- Fat 14.2 g
- Carbohydrates 12.5 g
- Sugar 1 g
- Protein 28 g
- Cholesterol 269 mg

Lemon Garlic Tilapia

Preparation Time: 10 minutes
Cooking Time: 10 minutes
Serve: 2

Ingredients:

- 2 tilapia fillets
- 1/2 tsp garlic powder
- 1/2 tsp onion powder
- 1/2 tsp lemon pepper seasoning
- Salt

Directions:

1. Season fish fillets with garlic powder, onion powder, lemon pepper seasoning, and salt.
2. Place fish fillets in the air fryer basket.
3. Select air fry then set the temperature to 360 F and time to 10 minutes. Press start.
4. Once the oven is preheated then place air fryer basket into the top rails of the oven.
5. Serve and enjoy.

Nutritional Value (Amount per Serving):

- Calories 226
- Fat 10 g
- Carbohydrates 3.3 g
- Sugar 2.4 g
- Protein 30.2 g
- Cholesterol 15 mg

Simple Cajun Salmon

Preparation Time: 10 minutes
Cooking Time: 8 minutes
Serve: 4

Ingredients:

- 4 salmon fillets
- 1 tsp Cajun seasoning
- 1/4 cup olive oil

Directions:

1. Brush salmon fillets with oil and season with Cajun seasoning.
2. Place salmon fillets in the air fryer basket.
3. Select air fry then set the temperature to 375 F and time to 8 minutes. Press start.
4. Once the oven is preheated then place air fryer basket into the top rails of the oven.
5. Serve and enjoy

Nutritional Value (Amount per Serving):

- Calories 343
- Fat 23.6 g
- Carbohydrates 0 g
- Sugar 0 g
- Protein 34.5 g
- Cholesterol 78 mg

Soy Honey Salmon

Preparation Time: 10 minutes
Cooking Time: 8 minutes
Serve: 4

Ingredients:

- 4 salmon fillets
- 2 tsp soy sauce
- 1 tbsp honey
- 1 tsp sesame seeds, toasted
- Pepper
- Salt

Directions:

1. Brush salmon with soy sauce and season with pepper and salt.
2. Place salmon in the air fryer basket.
3. Select air fry then set the temperature to 375 F and time to 8 minutes. Press start.
4. Once the oven is preheated then place air fryer basket into the top rails of the oven.
5. Brush salmon with honey and sprinkle with sesame seeds.
6. Serve and enjoy.

Nutritional Value (Amount per Serving):

- Calories 257
- Fat 11.4 g
- Carbohydrates 4.7 g
- Sugar 4.4 g
- Protein 34.9 g
- Cholesterol 78 mg

Salmon Cakes

Preparation Time: 10 minutes
Cooking Time: 7 minutes
Serve: 2

Ingredients:

- 1 egg, lightly beaten
- 8 oz salmon fillet, minced
- 1/4 tsp onion powder
- 1/4 tsp garlic powder
- Pepper
- Salt

Directions:

1. Add all ingredients into the bowl and mix until just combined.
2. Make small patties from the mixture and place onto the air fryer basket.
3. Select air fry then set the temperature to 400 F and time to 7 minutes. Press start.
4. Once the oven is preheated then place air fryer basket into the top rails of the oven.
5. Serve and enjoy.

Nutritional Value (Amount per Serving):

- Calories 185
- Fat 9 g
- Carbohydrates 1 g
- Sugar 0.5 g
- Protein 25 g
- Cholesterol 132 mg

Pesto Salmon

Preparation Time: 10 minutes
Cooking Time: 20 minutes
Serve: 4

Ingredients:

- 4 salmon fillets
- 1/2 cup basil pesto
- 2 cups grape tomatoes, halved
- 1 onion, chopped
- 1/2 cup feta cheese, crumbled

Directions:

1. Spray a baking dish with cooking spray and set aside.
2. Place salmon fillet in a baking dish and top with tomatoes, onion, pesto, and cheese.
3. Select bake then set the temperature to 350 F and time to 20 minutes. Press start.
4. Once the oven is preheated then place baking dish in the oven.
5. Serve and enjoy.

Nutritional Value (Amount per Serving):

- Calories 445
- Fat 25 g
- Carbohydrates 8 g
- Sugar 6 g
- Protein 41 g
- Cholesterol 103 mg

Delicious Cajun Salmon

Preparation Time: 10 minutes
Cooking Time: 12 minutes
Serve: 4

Ingredients:

- 4 salmon fillets
- 2 tsp Cajun seasoning
- 4 tbsp brown sugar
- Salt

Directions:

1. Mix Cajun seasoning, brown sugar, and salt and rub all over salmon.
2. Place salmon on the baking pan.
3. Select bake then set the temperature to 400 F and time to 12 minutes. Press start.
4. Once the oven is preheated then place baking pan in the oven.
5. Serve and enjoy.

Nutritional Value (Amount per Serving):

- Calories 270
- Fat 10 g
- Carbohydrates 8 g
- Sugar 8 g
- Protein 35 g
- Cholesterol 78 mg

Chapter 6: Vegetables & Side Dishes

Sweet & Spicy Cauliflower Florets

Preparation Time: 10 minutes

Cooking Time: 15 minutes

Serve: 6

Ingredients:

- 1 cauliflower head, cut into florets
- 1 tbsp cornstarch
- 2 tbsp olive oil
- 1 tbsp maple syrup
- 2 tbsp Sriracha

Directions:

1. In a mixing bowl, mix cornstarch, oil, maple syrup, and sriracha.
2. Add cauliflower florets into the mixing bowl and mix until well coated.
3. Arrange cauliflower florets to a sheet pan.
4. Select air fry then set the temperature to 375 F and time to 15 minutes. Press start.
5. Once the oven is preheated then place sheet pan in the oven.
6. Serve and enjoy.

Nutritional Value (Amount per Serving):

- Calories 91
- Fat 5 g
- Carbohydrates 11 g
- Sugar 8 g
- Protein 2 g
- Cholesterol 0 mg

Parmesan Mushrooms

Preparation Time: 10 minutes
Cooking Time: 15 minutes
Serve: 4

Ingredients:

- 1 lb mushrooms
- ¼ cup parmesan cheese, shredded
- 1 tsp Italian seasoning
- 1 tsp garlic powder
- 2 tbsp olive oil
- Pepper
- Sat

Directions:

1. In a bowl, toss mushrooms, Italian seasoning, garlic powder, oil, pepper, and salt.
2. Transfer mushrooms to air fryer basket.
3. Select air fry then set the temperature to 370 F and time to 13 minutes. Press start.
4. Once the oven is preheated then place air fryer basket into the top rails of the oven.
5. Sprinkle parmesan cheese over mushrooms and air fry for 2 minutes more.
6. Serve and enjoy.

Nutritional Value (Amount per Serving):

- Calories 105
- Fat 8 g
- Carbohydrates 6 g
- Sugar 2 g
- Protein 5 g
- Cholesterol 4 mg

Honey Baby Carrots

Preparation Time: 10 minutes
Cooking Time: 20 minutes
Serve: 4

Ingredients:

- 3 cups baby carrots
- 1 tbsp honey
- 1 tbsp olive oil
- Pepper
- Salt

Directions:

1. In a bowl, toss baby carrots with oil, honey, pepper, and salt.
2. Transfer carrots to air fryer basket.
3. Select air fry then set the temperature to 390 F and time to 15-20 minutes. Press start.
4. Once the oven is preheated then place air fryer basket into the top rails of the oven.
5. Serve and enjoy.

Nutritional Value (Amount per Serving):

- Calories 99
- Fat 3.5 g
- Carbohydrates 16.3 g
- Sugar 11.8 g
- Protein 0 g
- Cholesterol 0 mg

Delicious Corn Kernels

Preparation Time: 10 minutes
Cooking Time: 6 minutes
Serve: 6

Ingredients:

- 1 lb frozen corn
- 1 tbsp dried parsley
- 1 tbsp sugar
- ¼ cup butter

Directions:

1. Add corn, parsley, sugar, and butter into the baking dish and mix well.
2. Select air fry then set the temperature to 400 F and time to 6 minutes. Press start.
3. Once the oven is preheated then place baking dish into the oven. Stir corn after 3 minutes.
4. Serve and enjoy.

Nutritional Value (Amount per Serving):

- Calories 98
- Fat 8 g
- Carbohydrates 6.9 g
- Sugar 2.9 g
- Protein 0.9 g
- Cholesterol 20 mg

Squash & Zucchini

Preparation Time: 10 minutes
Cooking Time: 15 minutes
Serve: 6

Ingredients:

- 2 yellow squash, sliced
- 2 zucchini, sliced
- 1 tsp garlic, minced
- 1 tsp olive oil
- Pepper
- Salt

Directions:

1. In a bowl, toss squash and zucchini with garlic, oil, pepper, and salt.
2. Add squash and zucchini to air fryer basket.
3. Select air fry then set the temperature to 400 F and time to 15 minutes. Press start.
4. Once the oven is preheated then place air fryer basket into the top rails of the oven. Stir halfway through.
5. Serve and enjoy.

Nutritional Value (Amount per Serving):

- Calories 30
- Fat 1 g
- Carbohydrates 5 g
- Sugar 3 g
- Protein 2 g
- Cholesterol 0 mg

Brussels Sprouts & Sweet Potatoes

Preparation Time: 10 minutes

Cooking Time: 16 minutes

Serve: 6

Ingredients:

- 1 lb Brussels sprouts, cut in half
- 1 lb sweet potatoes, cut into 1/2-inch cubes
- 4 tbsp olive oil
- 1/2 tsp black pepper
- 1 tsp chili powder
- Pepper
- Salt

Directions:

1. Add sweet potatoes, Brussels sprouts, and remaining ingredients into the mixing bowl and toss well.
2. Transfer sweet potatoes and Brussels sprouts mixture to air fryer basket.
3. Select air fry then set the temperature to 380 F and time to 16 minutes. Press start.
4. Once the oven is preheated then place air fryer basket into the top rails of the oven. Stir halfway through.
5. Serve and enjoy.

Nutritional Value (Amount per Serving):

- Calories 204
- Fat 9.8 g
- Carbohydrates 28.3 g
- Sugar 2 g
- Protein 3.8 g
- Cholesterol 0 mg

Healthy Zucchini Patties

Preparation Time: 10 minutes
Cooking Time: 25 minutes
Serve: 6

Ingredients:

- 1 cup zucchini, shredded and squeeze out all liquid
- 2 tbsp onion, minced
- 1 egg, lightly beaten
- 1/4 tsp red pepper flakes
- 1/4 cup parmesan cheese, grated
- 1/2 tbsp Dijon mustard
- 1/2 tbsp mayonnaise
- 1/2 cup breadcrumbs
- Pepper
- Salt

Directions:

1. Add all ingredients into the bowl and mix until just combined.
2. Make small patties from the mixture and place onto the air fryer basket.
3. Select bake then set the temperature to 400 F and time to 25 minutes. Press start.
4. Once the oven is preheated then place air fryer basket into the top rails of the oven. Flip patties after 15 minutes.
5. Serve and enjoy.

Nutritional Value (Amount per Serving):

- Calories 156
- Fat 7.7 g
- Carbohydrates 7.9 g
- Sugar 1.2 g
- Protein 10.5 g
- Cholesterol 48 mg

Potato Carrot Roast

Preparation Time: 10 minutes
Cooking Time: 40 minutes
Serve: 2

Ingredients:

- 1/2 lb potatoes, cut into 1-inch cubes
- 1/2 onion, diced
- 1/2 tsp Italian seasoning
- 1/2 lb carrots, peeled & cut into chunks
- 1 tbsp olive oil
- 1/4 tsp garlic powder
- Pepper
- Salt

Directions:

1. In a large bowl, toss carrots, potatoes, garlic powder, Italian seasoning, oil, onion, pepper, and salt and transfer to air fryer basket.
2. Select bake then set the temperature to 400 F and time to 40 minutes. Press start.
3. Once the oven is preheated then place air fryer basket into the top rails of the oven. Stir halfway through.
4. Serve and enjoy.

Nutritional Value (Amount per Serving):

- Calories 201
- Fat 7.5 g
- Carbohydrates 32 g
- Sugar 8.2 g
- Protein 3.2 g
- Cholesterol 1 mg

Delicious Ranch Potatoes

Preparation Time: 10 minutes
Cooking Time: 20 minutes
Serve: 2

Ingredients:

- 1/2 lb baby potatoes, wash and cut in half
- 1/2 tbsp olive oil
- 1/4 tsp dill
- 1/4 tsp chives
- 1/4 tsp parsley
- 1/4 tsp smoked paprika
- 1/4 tsp onion powder
- 1/4 tsp garlic powder
- Salt

Directions:

1. Add all ingredients into the mixing bowl and toss well.
2. Spread potatoes to air fryer basket.
3. Select air fry then set the temperature to 400 F and time to 20 minutes. Press start.
4. Once the oven is preheated then place air fryer basket into the top rails of the oven. Stir halfway through.
5. Serve and enjoy.

Nutritional Value (Amount per Serving):

- Calories 99
- Fat 3.7 g
- Carbohydrates 14.8 g
- Sugar 0.2 g
- Protein 3.1 g
- Cholesterol 0 mg

Broccoli Fritters

Preparation Time: 10 minutes
Cooking Time: 30 minutes
Serve: 4

Ingredients:

- 3 cups broccoli florets, steam & chopped
- 2 eggs, lightly beaten
- 1/4 cup breadcrumbs
- 2 garlic cloves, minced
- 2 cups cheddar cheese, shredded
- Pepper
- Salt

Directions:

1. Add all ingredients into the bowl and mix until just combined.
2. Make small patties from the mixture and place onto the air fryer basket.
3. Select bake then set the temperature to 375 F and time to 30 minutes. Press start.
4. Once the oven is preheated then place air fryer basket into the top rails of the oven. Flip patties after 15 minutes.
5. Serve and enjoy.

Nutritional Value (Amount per Serving):

- Calories 311
- Fat 21.5 g
- Carbohydrates 10.8 g
- Sugar 2.1 g
- Protein 19.8 g
- Cholesterol 141 mg

Chapter 7: Snacks & Appetizers

Artichoke Spinach Dip

Preparation Time: 10 minutes
Cooking Time: 25 minutes
Serve: 12

Ingredients:

- 14 oz marinated artichoke hearts, chopped
- 10 oz spinach, chopped
- ½ cup gruyere cheese
- ½ cup parmesan cheese, shredded
- 1 ½ cups mozzarella cheese
- 1 tsp garlic, minced
- 1/3 cup mayonnaise
- 2/3 cup sour cream

Directions:

1. In a mixing bowl, add all ingredients and mix well.
2. Pour bowl mixture into the casserole dish.
3. Select bake then set the temperature to 375 F and time to 25 minutes. Press start.
4. Once the oven is preheated then place casserole dish into the oven.
5. Serve and enjoy.

Nutritional Value (Amount per Serving):

- Calories 290
- Fat 20 g
- Carbohydrates 15 g
- Sugar 2 g
- Protein 12 g
- Cholesterol 42 mg

Gooey Cheese Dip

Preparation Time: 10 minutes
Cooking Time: 20 minutes
Serve: 30

Ingredients:

- 8 oz cream cheese, softened
- 5 oz Asiago cheese
- 3 garlic cloves, minced
- 1 cup mozzarella cheese, shredded
- 1 cup sour cream

Directions:

1. In a bowl, add all ingredients and mix well.
2. Pour bowl mixture into the baking dish.
3. Select bake then set the temperature to 350 F and time to 20 minutes. Press start.
4. Once the oven is preheated then place baking dish into the oven.
5. Serve and enjoy.

Nutritional Value (Amount per Serving):

- Calories 69
- Fat 6 g
- Carbohydrates 2 g
- Sugar 1 g
- Protein 3 g
- Cholesterol 18 mg

Delicious Crab Dip

Preparation Time: 10 minutes
Cooking Time: 30 minutes
Serve: 30

Ingredients:

- 8 oz crab meat
- ¼ cup sour cream
- ¼ cup mayonnaise
- 1 tsp old bay seasoning
- 1 tsp garlic, minced
- ¼ cup Monterey jack cheese, shredded
- 2 tbsp parmesan cheese, grated
- 8 oz cream cheese
- ¼ tsp salt

Directions:

1. In a bowl, add all ingredients and mix well.
2. Pour bowl mixture into the greased baking pan.
3. Select bake then set the temperature to 350 F and time to 30 minutes. Press start.
4. Once the oven is preheated then place baking pan into the oven.
5. Serve and enjoy.

Nutritional Value (Amount per Serving):

- Calories 50
- Fat 5 g
- Carbohydrates 1 g
- Sugar 0 g
- Protein 2 g
- Cholesterol 17 mg

Savory Almonds

Preparation Time: 10 minutes
Cooking Time: 12 minutes
Serve: 6

Ingredients:

- 2 cups almonds
- ½ tsp garlic powder
- 1 tsp Italian seasoning
- 2 tsp rosemary, chopped
- 1 tbsp olive oil
- ½ tsp salt

Directions:

1. In a bowl, toss almonds with remaining ingredients.
2. Spread almonds onto the sheet pan.
3. Select bake then set the temperature to 350 F and time to 12 minutes. Press start.
4. Once the oven is preheated then place sheet pan into the oven.
5. Serve and enjoy.

Nutritional Value (Amount per Serving):

- Calories 208
- Fat 18.5 g
- Carbohydrates 7.3 g
- Sugar 1.5 g
- Protein 6.8 g
- Cholesterol 1 mg

Sweet & Spicy Pecans

Preparation Time: 10 minutes
Cooking Time: 10 minutes
Serve: 6

Ingredients:

- 2 cups pecan halves
- 2 tbsp brown sugar
- 3 tbsp butter, melted
- ½ tsp ground ginger
- ½ tsp cayenne
- 1 tsp cumin
- 2 tsp chili powder
- 1 tsp cinnamon
- 1 tsp salt

Directions:

1. Spread pecans onto the sheet pan.
2. Select bake then set the temperature to 400 F and time to 10 minutes. Press start.
3. Once the oven is preheated then place sheet pan into the oven.
4. In a mixing bowl, mix the remaining ingredients. Add pecans to the bowl and toss to coat.
5. Serve and enjoy.

Nutritional Value (Amount per Serving):

- Calories 348
- Fat 35.4 g
- Carbohydrates 9.4 g
- Sugar 4.4 g
- Protein 4.3 g
- Cholesterol 15 mg

Parmesan Carrot Fries

Preparation Time: 10 minutes
Cooking Time: 15 minutes
Serve: 4

Ingredients:

- 4 carrots, peeled and cut into fries
- 2 tbsp parmesan cheese, grated
- 1 1/2 tbsp garlic, minced
- 2 tbsp olive oil
- Pepper
- Salt

Directions:

1. Add carrots and remaining ingredients into the mixing bowl and toss well.
2. Spread carrots fries to air fryer basket.
3. Select air fry then set the temperature to 350 F and time to 15 minutes. Press start.
4. Once the oven is preheated then place air fryer basket into the top rails of the oven.
5. Serve and enjoy.

Nutritional Value (Amount per Serving):

- Calories 100
- Fat 7.6 g
- Carbohydrates 7.2 g
- Sugar 3 g
- Protein 1.6 g
- Cholesterol 2 mg

Easy Sweet Potato Fries

Preparation Time: 10 minutes
Cooking Time: 16 minutes
Serve: 2

Ingredients:

- 2 sweet potatoes, peeled and cut into fries shape
- 1/4 tsp paprika
- 1/4 tsp chili powder
- 1/2 tsp garlic powder
- 1 tbsp olive oil
- Salt

Directions:

1. In a bowl, add sweet potato fries, chili powder, garlic powder, olive oil, and salt and toss until well coated.
2. Spread sweet potato fries to air fryer basket.
3. Select bake then set the temperature to 380 F and time to 16 minutes. Press start.
4. Once the oven is preheated then place air fryer basket into the top rails of the oven. Stir-fries halfway through.
5. Serve and enjoy.

Nutritional Value (Amount per Serving):

- Calories 120
- Fat 7.1 g
- Carbohydrates 13.9 g
- Sugar 2.9 g
- Protein 1.2 g
- Cholesterol 0 mg

Tasty Potato Wedges

Preparation Time: 10 minutes
Cooking Time: 15 minutes
Serve: 4

Ingredients:

- 2 medium potatoes, cut into wedges
- 1/8 tsp cayenne pepper
- 1/4 tsp garlic powder
- 1/2 tsp paprika
- 1 1/2 tbsp olive oil
- 1/4 tsp pepper
- 1 tsp sea salt

Directions:

1. In a bowl, toss potato wedges with remaining ingredients.
2. Spread potato wedges to air fryer basket.
3. Select air fry then set the temperature to 400 F and time to 15 minutes. Press start.
4. Once the oven is preheated then place air fryer basket into the top rails of the oven. Stir halfway through.
5. Serve and enjoy.

Nutritional Value (Amount per Serving):

- Calories 121
- Fat 5 g
- Carbohydrates 17 g
- Sugar 1 g
- Protein 2 g
- Cholesterol 0 mg

Sweet Cinnamon Chickpeas

Preparation Time: 10 minutes
Cooking Time: 12 minutes
Serve: 4

Ingredients:

- 14.5 oz can chickpeas, rinsed, drained and pat dry
- 1 tbsp honey
- 1 tbsp olive oil
- 1/2 tsp ground cinnamon
- Pepper
- Salt

Directions:

1. Spread chickpeas onto the sheet pan.
2. Select air fry then set the temperature to 375 F and time to 12 minutes. Press start.
3. Once the oven is preheated then place the sheet pan in the oven.
4. In a large bowl, mix together cinnamon, honey, oil, pepper, and salt. Add chickpeas and toss well.
5. Serve and enjoy.

Nutritional Value (Amount per Serving):

- Calories 169
- Fat 4 g
- Carbohydrates 27 g
- Sugar 3 g
- Protein 5 g
- Cholesterol 0 mg

Salsa Cheese Dip

Preparation Time: 10 minutes
Cooking Time: 30 minutes
Serve: 10

Ingredients:

- 15 oz cream cheese, softened
- 1 cup sour cream
- 1/2 cup hot salsa
- 3 cups cheddar cheese, shredded

Directions:

1. In a mixing bowl, add all ingredients and mix well.
2. Pour bowl mixture into the casserole dish.
3. Select bake then set the temperature to 350 F and time to 25 minutes. Press start.
4. Once the oven is preheated then place casserole dish into the oven.
5. Serve and enjoy.

Nutritional Value (Amount per Serving):

- Calories 345
- Fat 32 g
- Carbohydrates 3.4 g
- Sugar 0.7 g
- Protein 12.8 g
- Cholesterol 96 mg

Parmesan Goat Cheese Dip

Preparation Time: 10 minutes
Cooking Time: 20 minutes
Serve: 8

Ingredients:

- 12 oz goat cheese
- 1/2 cup parmesan cheese, shredded
- 4 oz cream cheese
- 2 tsp rosemary, chopped
- 1 tsp red pepper flakes
- 4 garlic cloves, minced
- 2 tbsp olive oil
- 1/2 tsp salt

Directions:

1. In a mixing bowl, add all ingredients and mix well.
2. Pour bowl mixture into the casserole dish.
3. Select bake then set the temperature to 390 F and time to 20 minutes. Press start.
4. Once the oven is preheated then place casserole dish into the oven.
5. Serve and enjoy.

Nutritional Value (Amount per Serving):

- Calories 295
- Fat 25 g
- Carbohydrates 2.3 g
- Sugar 1 g
- Protein 16 g
- Cholesterol 64 mg

Spicy Walnuts

Preparation Time: 10 minutes
Cooking Time: 5 minutes
Serve: 6

Ingredients:

- 2 cups walnuts
- 1/4 tsp paprika
- 1 tsp olive oil
- 1/4 tsp chili powder
- Pepper
- Salt

Directions:

1. Add walnuts, paprika, chili powder, oil, pepper, and salt into the bowl and toss well.
2. Spread walnuts to air fryer basket.
3. Select air fry then set the temperature to 350 F and time to 5 minutes. Press start.
4. Once the oven is preheated then place air fryer basket into the top rails of the oven.
5. Serve and enjoy.

Nutritional Value (Amount per Serving):

- Calories 266
- Fat 25 g
- Carbohydrates 4 g
- Sugar 0.5 g
- Protein 10 g
- Cholesterol 0 mg

Flavorful Chicken Dip

Preparation Time: 10 minutes
Cooking Time: 25 minutes
Serve: 8

Ingredients:

- 2 chicken breasts, cooked and shredded
- 1/4 cup blue cheese, crumbled
- 1/2 cup ranch dressing
- 1/2 cup buffalo wing sauce
- 8 oz cream cheese, softened
- 1 cup mozzarella cheese, shredded
- 1 cup cheddar cheese, shredded

Directions:

1. In a mixing bowl, add all ingredients and mix well.
2. Pour bowl mixture into the casserole dish.
3. Select bake then set the temperature to 350 F and time to 25 minutes. Press start.
4. Once the oven is preheated then place casserole dish into the oven.
5. Serve and enjoy.

Nutritional Value (Amount per Serving):

- Calories 299
- Fat 23 g
- Carbohydrates 2 g
- Sugar 0.6 g
- Protein 20.8 g
- Cholesterol 94 mg

Lemon Ricotta Dip

Preparation Time: 10 minutes

Cooking Time: 15 minutes

Serve: 6

Ingredients:

- 1 cup ricotta cheese, shredded
- 1 tbsp lemon juice
- 1/4 cup parmesan cheese, grated
- 1/2 cup mozzarella cheese, shredded
- 2 tbsp olive oil
- 1 tsp garlic, minced
- Pepper
- Salt

Directions:

1. In a bowl, add all ingredients and mix well.
2. Pour bowl mixture into the casserole dish.
3. Select bake then set the temperature to 400 F and time to 15 minutes. Press start.
4. Once the oven is preheated then place casserole dish into the oven.
5. Serve and enjoy.

Nutritional Value (Amount per Serving):

- Calories 121
- Fat 9 g
- Carbohydrates 3 g
- Sugar 0.2 g
- Protein 6 g
- Cholesterol 17 mg

Cheesy Onion Dip

Preparation Time: 10 minutes
Cooking Time: 40 minutes
Serve: 8

Ingredients:

- 1 1/2 onions, chopped
- 1 cup mozzarella cheese, shredded
- 1/2 tsp garlic powder
- 1 1/2 cup Swiss cheese, shredded
- 1 cup cheddar cheese, shredded
- 1 1/2 cup mayonnaise
- Pepper
- Salt

Directions:

1. In a bowl, add all ingredients and mix well.
2. Pour bowl mixture into the casserole dish.
3. Select bake then set the temperature to 350 F and time to 40 minutes. Press start.
4. Once the oven is preheated then place casserole dish into the oven.
5. Serve and enjoy.

Nutritional Value (Amount per Serving):

- Calories 326
- Fat 25 g
- Carbohydrates 15 g
- Sugar 4 g
- Protein 10 g
- Cholesterol 47 mg

Chapter 8: Dehydrate

Cinnamon Apple Slices

Preparation Time: 10 minutes

Cooking Time: 8 hours

Serve: 3

Ingredients:

- 3 apples, core & slices ¼-inch thick
- ½ tsp vanilla
- ¼ tsp nutmeg
- 1 tsp cinnamon
- 1 tbsp sugar
- ½ lemon juice

Directions:

1. In a small bowl, mix vanilla, nutmeg, cinnamon, sugar, and lemon juice.
2. Arrange apple slices in the air fryer basket and brush with vanilla mixture.
3. Select dehydrate then set the temperature to 135 F and time to 8 hours. Press start.
4. Once the oven is preheated then place air fryer basket into the top rails of the oven.
5. Serve and enjoy.

Nutritional Value (Amount per Serving):

- Calories 136
- Fat 0.5 g
- Carbohydrates 35.6 g
- Sugar 27.4 g
- Protein 0.6 g
- Cholesterol 0 mg

Green Apple Slices

Preparation Time: 10 minutes

Cooking Time: 8 hours

Serve: 4

Ingredients:

- 3 green apples, cored & cut into ¼-inch thick slices
- 1 tsp cinnamon

Directions:

1. Arrange apple slices in the air fryer basket and sprinkle with cinnamon.
2. Select dehydrate then set the temperature to 145 F and time to 8 hours. Press start.
3. Once the oven is preheated then place air fryer basket into the top rails of the oven.
4. Serve and enjoy.

Nutritional Value (Amount per Serving):

- Calories 60
- Fat 0.2 g
- Carbohydrates 16 g
- Sugar 11 g
- Protein 0.3 g
- Cholesterol 0 mg

Eggplant Slices

Preparation Time: 10 minutes
Cooking Time: 4 hours
Serve: 4

Ingredients:

- 2 eggplants, cut into ¼-inch thick slices

Directions:

1. Arrange eggplant slices in the air fryer basket.
2. Select dehydrate then set the temperature to 145 F and time to 4 hours. Press start.
3. Once the oven is preheated then place air fryer basket into the top rails of the oven.
4. Serve and enjoy.

Nutritional Value (Amount per Serving):

- Calories 30
- Fat 0.2 g
- Carbohydrates 6.7 g
- Sugar 3.4 g
- Protein 1.1 g
- Cholesterol 0 mg

Zucchini Chips

Preparation Time: 10 minutes
Cooking Time: 8 hours
Serve: 4

Ingredients:

- 2 zucchini, cut into ¼-inch thick slices
- ¼ tsp garlic powder
- 1 tsp olive oil
- Pepper
- Salt

Directions:

1. In a bowl, toss zucchini slices with oil, garlic powder, pepper, and salt.
2. Arrange zucchini slices in the air fryer basket.
3. Select dehydrate then set the temperature to 135 F and time to 8 hours. Press start.
4. Once the oven is preheated then place air fryer basket into the top rails of the oven.
5. Serve and enjoy.

Nutritional Value (Amount per Serving):

- Calories 25
- Fat 1.4 g
- Carbohydrates 3.3 g
- Sugar 1.7 g
- Protein 1.2 g
- Cholesterol 0 mg

Banana Chips

Preparation Time: 10 minutes
Cooking Time: 6 hours
Serve: 4

Ingredients:

- 3 bananas, peel & cut into 1/8-inch thick slices

Directions:

1. Arrange banana slices in the air fryer basket.
2. Select dehydrate then set the temperature to 135 F and time to 6 hours. Press start.
3. Once the oven is preheated then place air fryer basket into the top rails of the oven.
4. Serve and enjoy.

Nutritional Value (Amount per Serving):

- Calories 106
- Fat 0.5 g
- Carbohydrates 27 g
- Sugar 14.4 g
- Protein 1.3 g
- Cholesterol 0 mg

Pear Slices

Preparation Time: 10 minutes
Cooking Time: 5 hours
Serve: 4

Ingredients:

- 3 pears, cut into ¼-inch thick slices

Directions:

1. Arrange banana slices in the air fryer basket.
2. Select dehydrate then set the temperature to 160 F and time to 5 hours. Press start.
3. Once the oven is preheated then place air fryer basket into the top rails of the oven.
4. Serve and enjoy.

Nutritional Value (Amount per Serving):

- Calories 60
- Fat 0.3 g
- Carbohydrates 16 g
- Sugar 10.2 g
- Protein 0.4 g
- Cholesterol 0 mg

Mushroom Slices

Preparation Time: 10 minutes

Cooking Time: 5 hours

Serve: 4

Ingredients:

- 1 ½ cups mushrooms, clean & cut into 1/8-inch thick slices

Directions:

1. Arrange mushroom slices in the air fryer basket.
2. Select dehydrate then set the temperature to 165 F and time to 5 hours. Press start.
3. Once the oven is preheated then place air fryer basket into the top rails of the oven.
4. Serve and enjoy.

Nutritional Value (Amount per Serving):

- Calories 6
- Fat 0.1 g
- Carbohydrates 0.6 g
- Sugar 0.3 g
- Protein 0.6 g
- Cholesterol 0 mg

Snap Pea Chips

Preparation Time: 10 minutes
Cooking Time: 8 hours
Serve: 4

Ingredients:

- 2 ½ cups snap peas
- ¼ tsp garlic powder
- 2 tsp olive oil
- Salt

Directions:

1. In a mixing bowl, add snap peas, oil, garlic powder, and salt and toss well.
2. Arrange snap peas to air fryer basket.
3. Select dehydrate then set the temperature to 135 F and time to 8 hours. Press start.
4. Once the oven is preheated then place air fryer basket into the top rails of the oven.
5. Serve and enjoy.

Nutritional Value (Amount per Serving):

- Calories 94
- Fat 2.7 g
- Carbohydrates 13.2 g
- Sugar 5 g
- Protein 5 g
- Cholesterol 0 mg

Dried Strawberries

Preparation Time: 10 minutes
Cooking Time: 6 hours
Serve: 4

Ingredients:

- 2 cups strawberries, cut into ¼-inch slices

Directions:

1. Arrange strawberry slices in the air fryer basket.
2. Select dehydrate then set the temperature to 160 F and time to 6 hours. Press start.
3. Once the oven is preheated then place air fryer basket into the top rails of the oven.
4. Serve and enjoy.

Nutritional Value (Amount per Serving):

- Calories 23
- Fat 0.2 g
- Carbohydrates 5.5 g
- Sugar 3.5 g
- Protein 0.5 g
- Cholesterol 0mg

Lemon Slices

Preparation Time: 10 minutes
Cooking Time: 10 hours
Serve: 6

Ingredients:

- 6 lemon, cut into ¼-inch thick slices

Directions:

1. Arrange lemon slices in the air fryer basket.
2. Select dehydrate then set the temperature to 125 F and time to 10 hours. Press start.
3. Once the oven is preheated then place air fryer basket into the top rails of the oven.
4. Serve and enjoy.

Nutritional Value (Amount per Serving):

- Calories 17
- Fat 0.2 g
- Carbohydrates 5.4 g
- Sugar 1.5 g
- Protein 0.6 g
- Cholesterol 0 mg

Chapter 9: Desserts

Raspberry Muffins

Preparation Time: 10 minutes
Cooking Time: 35 minutes
Serve: 6

Ingredients:

- 2 eggs
- 3 oz raspberries
- 2 tbsp butter, melted
- 2 tbsp honey
- 1 tsp baking powder
- 5 oz almond flour

Directions:

1. Line 6-cup muffin tray with cupcake liners and set aside.
2. In a bowl, mix almond flour and baking powder.
3. Add honey, eggs, and butter and stir until just combined.
4. Add raspberries and fold well.
5. Spoon batter into the prepared muffin tray.
6. Select bake then set the temperature to 350 F and time to 35 minutes. Press start.
7. Once the oven is preheated then place muffin tray in the oven.
8. Serve and enjoy.

Nutritional Value (Amount per Serving):

- Calories 225
- Fat 18 g
- Carbohydrates 13 g
- Sugar 7 g
- Protein 7 g
- Cholesterol 55 mg

Healthy Carrot Muffins

Preparation Time: 10 minutes
Cooking Time: 20 minutes
Serve: 6

Ingredients:

- 1 egg
- 1/4 cup light brown sugar
- 1/4 cup granulated sugar
- 1/2 tbsp canola oil
- 1 1/2 tsp baking powder
- 1/4 tsp nutmeg
- 1 tsp cinnamon
- 1 cup all-purpose flour
- 3/4 cup grated carrots
- 1 tsp vanilla
- 1/4 cup applesauce
- 1/4 tsp salt

Directions:

1. Line 6-cup muffin tray with cupcake liners and set aside.
2. Add all ingredients into the bowl and mix until well combined.
3. Pour batter into the prepared muffin tray.
4. Select bake then set the temperature to 350 F and time to 20 minutes. Press start.
5. Once the oven is preheated then place muffin tray in the oven.
6. Serve and enjoy.

Nutritional Value (Amount per Serving):

- Calories 166
- Fat 2 g
- Carbohydrates 33 g
- Sugar 15 g
- Protein 3 g
- Cholesterol 27 mg

Easy Baked Pears

Preparation Time: 10 minutes
Cooking Time: 25 minutes
Serve: 4

Ingredients:

- 4 pears, cut in half and core
- 6 tbsp maple syrup
- 1/2 tsp vanilla
- 1/4 tsp cinnamon

Directions:

1. Arrange pears, cut side up in the greased baking dish, and sprinkle with cinnamon.
2. In a small bowl, whisk vanilla and maple syrup and drizzle over pears.
3. Select bake then set the temperature to 375 F and time to 25 minutes. Press start.
4. Once the oven is preheated then place baking dish into the oven.
5. Serve and enjoy.

Nutritional Value (Amount per Serving):

- Calories 224
- Fat 0.4 g
- Carbohydrates 58 g
- Sugar 44 g
- Protein 0.8 g
- Cholesterol 0 mg

Healthy & Easy Brownie

Preparation Time: 10 minutes

Cooking Time: 10 minutes

Serve: 2

Ingredients:

- 1 egg, lightly beaten
- 1/2 tsp vanilla
- 1/4 cup maple syrup
- 1/2 cup sun butter
- 2 tbsp coconut flour
- 2 tbsp cocoa powder
- 1/4 tsp salt

Directions:

1. In a bowl, combine together sun butter, egg, vanilla, maple syrup, and salt.
2. Add coconut flour and cocoa powder and stir to combine.
3. Pour mixture into the greased baking dish.
4. Select bake then set the temperature to 350 F and time to 10 minutes. Press start.
5. Once the oven is preheated then place baking dish into the oven.
6. Serve and enjoy.

Nutritional Value (Amount per Serving):

- Calories 609
- Fat 37 g
- Carbohydrates 51 g
- Sugar 30 g
- Protein 19 g
- Cholesterol 82 mg

Almond Cookies

Preparation Time: 10 minutes
Cooking Time: 25 minutes
Serve: 15

Ingredients:

- 1 egg
- 1 tsp liquid stevia
- 2 cups almond flour
- 1 tsp cinnamon
- 1 tsp vanilla
- 1/2 cup butter, softened

Directions:

1. In a large bowl, add all ingredients and mix until well combined.
2. Make cookies from mixture and place on a parchment-lined sheet pan.
3. Select bake then set the temperature to 300 F and time to 25 minutes. Press start.
4. Once the oven is preheated then place sheet pan into the oven.
5. Serve and enjoy.

Nutritional Value (Amount per Serving):

- Calories 80
- Fat 8 g
- Carbohydrates 1 g
- Sugar 0.2 g
- Protein 1.2 g
- Cholesterol 27 mg

Tasty Pumpkin Cookies

Preparation Time: 10 minutes
Cooking Time: 25 minutes
Serve: 27

Ingredients:

- 1 egg
- 1/2 tsp pumpkin pie spice
- 2 cups almond flour
- 1/2 tsp baking powder
- 1 tsp vanilla
- 1/2 cup butter
- 1/2 cup pumpkin puree
- 1 tsp liquid stevia

Directions:

1. In a large bowl, add all ingredients and mix until well combined.
2. Make small cookies from the mixture and place on a parchment-lined sheet pan.
3. Select bake then set the temperature to 300 F and time to 25 minutes. Press start.
4. Once the oven is preheated then place sheet pan into the oven.
5. Serve and enjoy.

Nutritional Value (Amount per Serving):

- Calories 45
- Fat 4 g
- Carbohydrates 1 g
- Sugar 0.3 g
- Protein 0.7 g
- Cholesterol 15 mg

Delicious Brownie

Preparation Time: 10 minutes
Cooking Time: 20 minutes
Serve: 8

Ingredients:

- 2 eggs
- 1 tsp vanilla
- 1 1/4 cup brown sugar
- 1 cup butter, melted
- 1/2 cup chocolate chips
- 2 cup all-purpose flour
- 2 tsp baking powder
- 1/2 tsp salt

Directions:

1. In a bowl, mix melted butter and sugar. Add vanilla and eggs and mix well.
2. Add flour, baking powder, and salt and mix until well combined. Add chocolate chips and stir well.
3. Pour batter into the greased baking dish.
4. Select bake then set the temperature to 350 F and time to 20 minutes. Press start.
5. Once the oven is preheated then place baking dish into the oven.
6. Serve and enjoy.

Nutritional Value (Amount per Serving):

- Calories 480
- Fat 27.5 g
- Carbohydrates 53.1 g
- Sugar 28 g
- Protein 6 g
- Cholesterol 104 mg

Cream Cheese Muffins

Preparation Time: 10 minutes
Cooking Time: 16 minutes
Serve: 8

Ingredients:

- 2 eggs
- 1/2 cup Swerve
- 8 oz cream cheese
- 1 tsp ground cinnamon
- 1/2 tsp vanilla

Directions:

1. In a bowl, mix together cream cheese, vanilla, Swerve, and eggs until soft.
2. Pour batter into the silicone muffin molds and sprinkle cinnamon on top.
3. Select bake then set the temperature to 325 F and time to 16 minutes. Press start.
4. Once the oven is preheated then place silicone molds into the oven.
5. Serve and enjoy.

Nutritional Value (Amount per Serving):

- Calories 116
- Fat 11 g
- Carbohydrates 1.2 g
- Sugar 0.2 g
- Protein 3.5 g
- Cholesterol 72 mg

Tasty Raspberry Cobbler

Preparation Time: 10 minutes
Cooking Time: 10 minutes
Serve: 6

Ingredients:

- 1 egg, lightly beaten
- 1 cup raspberries, sliced
- 1 tbsp butter, melted
- 1 cup almond flour
- 2 tsp swerve
- 1/2 tsp vanilla

Directions:

1. Add raspberries to the baking dish.
2. Sprinkle sweetener over raspberries.
3. Mix almond flour, vanilla, and butter in the bowl.
4. Add egg in almond flour mixture and stir well to combine.
5. Spread almond flour mixture over sliced raspberries.
6. Select bake then set the temperature to 350 F and time to 10 minutes. Press start.
7. Once the oven is preheated then place baking dish into the oven.
8. Serve and enjoy.

Nutritional Value (Amount per Serving):

- Calories 65
- Fat 5 g
- Carbohydrates 3 g
- Sugar 1 g
- Protein 2 g
- Cholesterol 32 mg

Easy Scalloped Pineapple

Preparation Time: 10 minutes
Cooking Time: 35 minutes
Serve: 6

Ingredients:

- 3 eggs, lightly beaten
- 8 oz can crushed pineapple, un-drained
- 1/4 cup milk
- 1/2 cup butter, melted
- 2 cups of sugar
- 4 cups of bread cubes

Directions:

1. In a bowl, whisk eggs with milk, butter, crushed pineapple, and sugar.
2. Add bread cubes and stir well to coat.
3. Transfer mixture to the greased baking dish.
4. Select bake then set the temperature to 350 F and time to 35 minutes. Press start.
5. Once the oven is preheated then place baking dish into the oven.
6. Serve and enjoy.

Nutritional Value (Amount per Serving):

- Calories 511
- Fat 16 g
- Carbohydrates 85 g
- Sugar 70 g
- Protein 3.4 g
- Cholesterol 123 mg

Chapter 10: 30-Day Meal Plan

Day 1

Breakfast- Jalapeno Egg Muffins

Lunch- Nutritious Chicken & Veggies

Dinner- Tasty Steak Bites

Day 2

Breakfast- Banana Oatmeal Muffins

Lunch- Delicious Cajun Salmon

Dinner- Beef & Broccoli

Day 3

Breakfast- Coconut Pineapple Oatmeal

Lunch- Healthy Chicken Patties

Dinner- Juicy Baked Burger Patties

Day 4

Breakfast- Delicious Breakfast Potatoes

Lunch- Shrimp with Veggies

Dinner- Ranch Pork Chops

Day 5

Breakfast- Soft & Fluffy Strawberry Donuts

Lunch- Crispy Chicken Thighs

Dinner- Easy Pork Ribs

Day 6

Breakfast- Egg Sweet Potato Hash Muffins

Lunch- Shrimp Fajitas

Dinner- Greek Lamb Chops

Day 7

Breakfast- Bacon Egg Breakfast Casserole

Lunch- Juicy & Tasty Chicken Breasts

Dinner- Ranch Pork Chops

Day 8

Breakfast- French Toast Sticks

Lunch- Quick & Easy Shrimp Boil

Dinner- Herb Lamb Cutlets

Day 9

Breakfast- Baked Omelet

Lunch- Flavorful Chicken Fajitas

Dinner- Tasty Beef Tips

Day 10

Breakfast- Healthy Tofu Egg Muffins

Lunch- Soy Honey Salmon

Dinner- Greek Lamb Chops

Day 11

Breakfast- Jalapeno Egg Muffins

Lunch- Lemon Garlic Tilapia

Dinner- Easy Mustard Lamb Chops

Day 12

Breakfast- Banana Oatmeal Muffins

Lunch- Easy Cajun Shrimp with Veggies

Dinner- Flavorful Beef Fajitas

Day 13

Breakfast- Coconut Pineapple Oatmeal

Lunch- Parmesan Shrimp

Dinner- Parmesan Pork Chops

Day 14

Breakfast- Delicious Breakfast Potatoes

Lunch- Easy Shrimp Casserole

Dinner- Herb Lamb Chops

Day 15

Breakfast- Soft & Fluffy Strawberry Donuts

Lunch- Pesto Salmon

Dinner- Parmesan Pork Chops

Day 16

Breakfast- Jalapeno Egg Muffins

Lunch- Nutritious Chicken & Veggies

Dinner- Tasty Steak Bites

Day 17

Breakfast- Banana Oatmeal Muffins

Lunch- Delicious Cajun Salmon

Dinner- Beef & Broccoli

Day 18

Breakfast- Coconut Pineapple Oatmeal

Lunch- Healthy Chicken Patties

Dinner- Juicy Baked Burger Patties

Day 19

Breakfast- Delicious Breakfast Potatoes

Lunch- Shrimp with Veggies

Dinner- Ranch Pork Chops

Day 20

Breakfast- Soft & Fluffy Strawberry Donuts

Lunch- Crispy Chicken Thighs

Dinner- Easy Pork Ribs

Day 21

Breakfast- Egg Sweet Potato Hash Muffins

Lunch- Shrimp Fajitas

Dinner- Greek Lamb Chops

Day 22

Breakfast- Bacon Egg Breakfast Casserole

Lunch- Juicy & Tasty Chicken Breasts

Dinner- Ranch Pork Chops

Day 23

Breakfast- French Toast Sticks

Lunch- Quick & Easy Shrimp Boil

Dinner- Herb Lamb Cutlets

Day 24

Breakfast- Baked Omelet

Lunch- Flavorful Chicken Fajitas

Dinner- Tasty Beef Tips

Day 25

Breakfast- Healthy Tofu Egg Muffins

Lunch- Soy Honey Salmon

Dinner- Greek Lamb Chops

Day 26

Breakfast- Jalapeno Egg Muffins

Lunch- Lemon Garlic Tilapia

Dinner- Easy Mustard Lamb Chops

Day 27

Breakfast- Banana Oatmeal Muffins

Lunch- Easy Cajun Shrimp with Veggies

Dinner- Flavorful Beef Fajitas

Day 28

Breakfast- Coconut Pineapple Oatmeal

Lunch- Parmesan Shrimp

Dinner- Parmesan Pork Chops

Day 29

Breakfast- Delicious Breakfast Potatoes

Lunch- Easy Shrimp Casserole

Dinner- Herb Lamb Chops

Day 30

Breakfast- Soft & Fluffy Strawberry Donuts

Lunch- Pesto Salmon

Dinner- Parmesan Pork Chops

Conclusion

The Ninja Foodi Digital Air Fryer Oven is one of the hottest kitchen gadgets available in the market. It is not just an electric oven. It is the combination of oven, air fryer, and toaster which makes Ninja Foodi is a multipurpose cooking appliance. It is loaded with 8 programmable functions like Air fry, Air Roast, Air Broil, Toast, keep warm, Dehydrate, Bake, and Bagel. Ninja is one of the strong competitors of instant pot for making advanced multipurpose cooking appliances.

The cookbook contains 100 different types of healthy and delicious recipes written from breakfast, main meal to deserts. All the recipes written in this cookbook are unique and choose from globally inspired dishes. The recipes are written in an easily understandable form and written with their preparation and cooking time. Every recipe written in this book ends with their actual nutritional value information.

CPSIA information can be obtained
at www.ICGtesting.com
Printed in the USA
BVHW081322121121
621384BV00010BA/141